THE MYSTERY OF THE EUCHARIST
IN THE ANGLICAN TRADITION

H. R. McAdoo was Archbishop of Dublin and Primate of Ireland until his retirement in 1985. He was co-chairman of ARCIC I during the lifetime of the Commission and was chairman of the Holy Communion sub-committee of the Liturgical Advisory Committee of the Church of Ireland which produced the *Alternative Prayer Book* (1984). An Honorary Fellow of Trinity College, Dublin, his publications include: *The Structure of Caroline Moral Theology* (London 1949); *The Spirit of Anglicanism* (London and New York 1965); *Modern Eucharistic Agreement* (London 1973); *The Unity of Anglicanism: Catholic and Reformed* (Connecticut 1983); *The Eucharistic Theology of Jeremy Taylor Today* (Norwich 1988); *Anglican Heritage: Theology and Spirituality* (Norwich 1991); *First of Its Kind: Jeremy Taylor's Life of Christ – A Study in the Functioning of a Moral Theology* (Norwich 1994). He has also contributed to *Der Priesterliche Dienst V* (ed. H. Vorgrimler, Freiburg 1973); *The Anglican Moral Choice* (ed. Paul Elmen, Connecticut 1983); *Authority in the Anglican Commission* (ed. S. Sykes, Toronto 1987); *Christian Authority* (ed. G. R. Evans, Oxford 1988); *The English Religious Tradition and the Genius of Anglicanism* (ed. Geoffrey Rowell, Ikon 1992).

Kenneth Stevenson has been Rector of Holy Trinity and St Mary's Guildford since 1986, before which he was Chaplain and Lecturer in Liturgy at Manchester University. He is a member of the Liturgical Commission of the Church of England, and of the faith and order Advisory Group; he was born a Scottish Episcopalian and is also Secretary of the Anglo-Nordic-Baltic Theological Conference. He has written a number of books in the field of Liturgy and Sacramental Theology, which include *Nuptial Blessing: A Study of Christian Marriage Rites* (1982); *Eucharist and Offering* (1986); *To Join Together* (1987); *Jerusalem Revisited* (on the Holy Week Liturgies) (1988); *The First Rites* (on early Christian worship, arising from a series of BBC Television programmes) (1989); a collection of articles on liturgical and theological subjects, *Worship: Wonderful and the Sacred Mystery* (1992); and a study of the eucharistic theology of the 17th century Anglican Divines, *Covenant of Grace Renewed* (1994). He has contributed to several theological journals, and also to a number of collections of essays, including *Thomas Cranmer: Essays in Commemoration of the 500th Anniversary of his Birth* (1990), *Thomas Cranmer: Churchman and Scholar* (1993), *Winchester Cathedral: Nine Hundred Years* (1993), and *Le Mariage: Conférences Saint Serge XLe Semaine d'Etudes Liturgiques, Paris 1993* (1994). He has edited *Liturgy Reshaped* (1982) and coedited, with Bryan Spinks, *The Identity of Anglican Worship* (1992). He took part in the study-group and helped to edit, and contributed to the volume of essays resulting in *Heritage and Prophecy: Grundtvig and the English-Speaking World* (1994).

What Happens at Holy Communion?

THE MYSTERY OF THE EUCHARIST IN THE ANGLICAN TRADITION

by

H. R. McAdoo and Kenneth W. Stevenson

FOREWORD BY
ROWAN WILLIAMS
Bishop of Monmouth

The Canterbury Press
Norwich

First published 1995 by The Canterbury Press Norwich
(a publishing imprint of Hymns Ancient & Modern Limited
a registered charity)
St Mary's Works, St Mary's Plain,
Norwich, Norfolk, NR3 3BH

British Library Cataloguing in Publication Data

A catalogue record for this book is available
from the British Library

ISBN 1–85311–113–9

*Typeset by Waveney Studios
Diss, Norfolk
and printed in Great Britain by
St Edmundsbury Press Limited
Bury St Edmunds, Suffolk*

Presence and Sacrifice: 'Both are areas of "mystery" which ultimately defy definition'.

(*The Report of the Lambeth Conference 1988*)

Foreword

Recent years have seen much debate in Anglican circles about the Eucharist. Liturgical revision has, inevitably, focused attention on what looks like unfinished business in Anglican eucharistic theology; the ARCIC process has re-opened the question of whether the division between Anglican and Tridentine thinking about the Eucharist follows precisely the lines taken for granted three hundred years ago; the ordination of women to the priesthood in many Anglican provinces raises some awkward questions about what is central or essential in the 'doing' of the Eucharist; and the recent pressure in some evangelical circles for the licensing of lay celebration has caused similar anxiety.

If we look at the way practically all of these controversies have been conducted, one thing that immediately strikes the observer who has any awareness of Anglican history is the phenomenal degree of collective amnesia on this general subject that seems to afflict Anglicans. To listen to some people, you might never guess that the Anglican church had ever had a theology of ministry and sacraments in any way distant from that of the post-Tridentine Roman Catholic Church. To listen to others, you could be forgiven for thinking that appeal to New Testament practice (at least as reconstructed on the basis of a number of arguments from silence) settled all disputes of doctrine and discipline in the Communion. But the truth of the matter is that enormous energies were devoted, up to the middle of the nineteenth century at least, to establishing that neither of these positions was adequate. Victorian controversy still skews our perceptions of Anglican history more than we realise, whether we think of ourselves as 'Catholic' or 'Reformed' in our Anglican loyalties. At the moment, a lot of Anglicans are aware of something of a crisis over the location of Anglican identity; and if we, in consequence, start working at overcoming our amnesia, it is not for antiquarian reasons, but because the constant rehearsing of essentially nineteenth century polemical battles within the Anglican conversation is proving increasingly sterile – not to say ecumenically paralysing and frustrating.

Both the authors of this book have a noble record in the battle against Anglican amnesia; and in this vastly learned and yet very readable work, they have succeeded in uncovering not only a range of Anglican thinking on the Eucharist, but a profound underlying *coherence* in that thinking. What seems to come across most clearly here is that in theologising both about sacrifice and about presence in the Eucharist, Anglican writing of the 'classical' period, and indeed of later periods as well, has returned with a sure instinct to a vision of the centrality of Christ's *personal action* in the Eucharist. In respect of sacrifice, what is definitive is, as has often been noted, a stress upon the heavenly prayer of Christ. The glorified Christ, crucified and risen, is eternally active towards God the Father on our behalf, drawing us into the eternal movement of self-giving love that the Son or Word directs towards the source of all, the God Jesus calls 'Abba'. The sacrifice of the cross in history is, among other things, the 'transcription' into this world's terms of the Son's movement of love towards the Father in heaven. In the Eucharist, our prayer is swept into that current, and we are set free to share the Son's self-giving. The giving of thanks over the elements renews for us the covenant made by God in Christ, and the work of God in the cross is again 'applied' to us, in word and action, in body and soul.

Thus the presence that is appropriate and intelligible in the Eucharist is neither the presence of an idea in our minds (a notion most of the British Reformers of the first few generations would have found very odd), nor the presence of a uniquely sacred *object* on the Table. It is the presence of an active Christ, moving in love not only towards the Father but towards us. The more we try to 'immobilise' Christ, either in heaven (so that all that happens at the Eucharist happens in our minds) or in substantial presence on an altar (so that his action is virtually completed in simply being there under the sacramental forms), the less we understand of the dynamism of the sacrament, and of the transfiguring liberty of the risen Christ. For if we look first to Christ in the Eucharist as active, we can see how sacrifice and presence together make sense. The offering of the love of the Son in his incarnate life and bloody death is woven into the eternal life of the Trinity; when the crucified Son is raised from the dead, we understand that the sacrifice lived by Jesus and consummated in the cross is an abiding reality, an indestructible life and an inexhaustible gift. And the great mark of discipleship to the risen Christ is, as the New Testament has it, that we eat and drink with him after his resurrection: the love given to the Father is given to us who receive his hospitality.

Something of this is what pervades the Anglican tradition of thought about the Eucharist. Of course, it is echoed in all kinds of ways by Roman Catholic, Byzantine and Reformed divines, past and present; but there is still something distinctive in the quite single-minded focus of so many Anglican writers upon the active Christ – a focus that allows them a fair bit of scepticism about theories of presence and sacrifice at times, not out of native intellectual laziness but out of a very proper conviction that most tidy theories here will obscure the force and urgency of Christ's action – what George Herbert, in a poem on the Eucharist not published until 1874, wonderfully calls, 'The haste of Thy good will'.

Here, then, is a deeply welcome book, significant for the ecumenical enterprise (because we need to bring into that enterprise what is best and clearest in our past) and for the renewal of a serious, reflective and literate Anglicanism. The little irony that this book is written by scholars formed in the Scottish and Irish provinces (and that this introduction is written by a member of the Church in Wales) might even be an encouragement to those who need reminding that Anglicanism is not after all simply a bit of the English Heritage industry. It has a voice with integrity, worth recovering for the health of the present-day Anglican Communion and of the wider family of the Church Catholic.

ROWAN WILLIAMS

Contents

PART ONE

THE MYSTERY OF PRESENCE

H. R. McAdoo

I

What Happens at Holy Communion? Anglican Answers

'The manna is a type of the spiritual food which by the resurrection of the Lord became a reality in the mystery of the Eucharist'
(From an unknown fourth century author)

If this section were to have an explanatory subtitle it might well be *'Theological reflections on the Mystery of the Eucharist'*. From earliest times Christians have seen the eucharist as ultimately within a perspective of mystery whether it be in terms of the spiritual feeding of the communicant or of the instrumental efficacy of the elements or of the *anamnesis* of the once-for-all sacrifice made actual in the eucharist and presented to the Father in and with the continual intercession of the risen and glorified Christ. It is not only the Eastern Orthodox but the Book of Common Prayer and generations of Anglican theologians who describe the eucharist and the elements as *'these holy mysteries'*.

There is a feeling of wonder, a recognition that we cannot understand everything or encapsulate it in a definition, a sense that what inspires our wonder is something real though words cannot capture it. Basically, this is what is conveyed by the word 'mystery'. As the poet Gerard Manley Hopkins put it, mystery for the Christian means an incomprehensible certainty not an interesting uncertainty. In everyday language, a mystery is something inexplicable, a secret to which the explanation has not been found. In the New Testament we find a different emphasis as when St Paul speaks of 'the

3

mystery of the Gospel' and writes of 'the mystery that has
been kept hidden for ages and generations, but is now disclosed to the saints. To them God has chosen to make known
among the Gentiles the glorious riches of this mystery, which
is Christ in you, the hope of glory' (Col. 1.26–7). This is saying that the mystery is a secret in the process of being disclosed by God in the experience of men and women, for the
mystery of the Gospel is what God has revealed and is revealing in and through Christ. (cp. Rom. 16.25–6) The same line
of thought is apparent in the epistle to the Ephesians (1.9):
'He made known to us the mystery of his will according to
his good pleasure, which he purposed in Christ'. Indeed, my
dictionary more or less confirms this interpretation since it
reads as two meanings of the word mystery: 'Christianity,
any truth that is divinely revealed but otherwise unknowable.
Christianity, a sacramental rite, such as the Eucharist, or
(when pl.) the consecrated elements of the Eucharist', which
brings us back to 'the holy mysteries'. It is noteworthy that
modern eucharistic agreements such as the *Windsor Statement* (3), (6) and *Elucidation* (7) of ARCIC I and *The Lima
Report of the WCC, Commentary* (13), (15) underline the
mystery of what happens at Holy Communion.

Probably this chimes with the feelings and experience of
many faithful communicants, even a majority of them, and
Thomas Ken (1637–1711) whose hymns we sing after three
centuries might well speak for them all: 'Lord, what need I
labour in vain to search out the manner of thy mysterious
presence in the sacrament, when my love assures me thou art
there?' and 'I believe thy body and blood to be as really present in the Holy Sacrament, as thy divine power can make it,
though the manner of thy mysterious presence I cannot comprehend'.[1] They would say Amen to Richard Hooker's
(1554?–1600) plea: 'Shall I wish that men would give themselves more to meditate with silence what we have by the
sacrament, and less to dispute of the manner How?'[2] Yet still,
'the manner of the mysterious presence', 'the manner How',

has preoccupied those who affirm the *mysterium fidei* but who seek legitimately, to strengthen faith in terms of apprehending and making their own what has been revealed, or who seek, illegitimately, to exclude others by mandatory definitions. The history of Christian eucharistic theology sadly confirms Jeremy Taylor (1613–1667) who, viewing the discords and debates on the manner of Christ's presence in the eucharist, wrote 'The tree of life is now become an apple of contention'.[3]

If for Christians a mystery is something in the process of being disclosed by God but 'because it is a *divine* secret it remains mystery and does not become transparent to men',[4] it must be legitimate to attempt to uncover elements or concepts which enable us, so to speak, to reach on the mystery, to be open intellectually and spiritually to its thrust, for 'the spirit in man is the candle of the Lord' and a mystery of faith is not a muddle or a mess but *an unexplained yet experienced reality*. Here we call to mind Jeremy Taylor's *The Worthy Communicant* (1660) in the introduction of which this same point is handled. As we approach 'this great mysterious feast and magazine of grace' we are made aware that 'Christ comes to meet us, clothed with a mystery: he hath a house below as well as above ... the Church and the holy table of the Lord ... the word and the sacrament, the oblation of bread and wine, and the offering of ourselves'. There are however practical implications: because 'the sacraments are mysteries and to be handled by mystic persons ... therefore, whoever will partake of God's secrets, must first look into his own; he must pare off whatsoever is amiss'. The Christian must search his state and his conscience and he must not expect to discern all that is in this 'cloud' since 'the holy communion ... is the most sacred, mysterious, and useful conjugation of secret and holy things and duties in the religion. It is not easy to be understood ... it is not much opened in the writings of the New Testament, but still left in its mysterious nature'.

Where then does this leave us, asks Taylor? Some theologians, in his view, have twisted the mystery making it
'intricate by explications, and difficult by the aperture and
dissolution of distinctions'. The consequences are clear in the
history of the Church and of Christian doctrine: 'this great
mystery of our religion, in which some espy strange things
which God intended not, and others see not what God hath
plainly told: some call that part of it a mystery which is none:
and others think all of it nothing but a mere ceremony and a
sign: some say it signifies, and some say it effects: some say it
is a sacrifice, and others call it a sacrament' and all come to
it for an infinite variety of needs and reasons. His own purpose however is to relate the eucharistic mystery to where the
Christian is and to where he hopes by grace to be, becoming
what he really is. His intent is 'not to dispute, but to persuade
... to instruct those that need'. His design therefore is 'to
gather together into a union all those several portions of
truth, and *differing apprehensions of mysteriousness*' with
a view to their impact on Christian living: 'the differing opinions, and several understandings of this mystery, which (it
may be) no human understanding can comprehend, will serve
to excellent purposes of the Spirit'. Always Taylor is a moral/
ascetical theologian and though the Mystery of the Eucharist
is 'ineffable' it can never be separated from the experienced
reality of Christian discipleship. The mystery is God's secret
and self-disclosure and 'Christ comes to meet us, clothed
with a mystery' but 'if I describe the excellencies of this sacrament, I find it engages us upon matters of duty, and inquiries
practical: if I describe our duty, it plainly signifies the greatness and excellency of the mystery'. He goes to the heart of
the New Testament understanding of our 'knowledge in the
mystery of Christ' (Eph. 3.4) and of 'the mystery of godliness:
God was manifest in the flesh' (1 Tim. 3.16) when he simply
affirms that 'we cannot discourse of the secret, but by describing our duty; and we cannot draw all the lines of duty,
but so much duty must needs open a cabinet of mysteries'.[5]

The Orthodox theologian, Olivier Clément, in his *The Roots of Christian Mysticism* (1993), has demonstrated with numerous examples how deeply embedded this concept of 'the mystery of Christ' (Eph. 3.4) is in a wide range of patristic theology and devotion. 'In Jesus, however', he writes, 'the mystery is at the same time disclosed and veiled' and he shows in passage after passage how this pervades and penetrates the thought of the early writers: 'He was sent not only to be recognized but also to remain hidden' (*Origen*); 'Christ is the great hidden mystery ...', 'He remains hidden ... even in this disclosure' (*Maximus the Confessor*); 'In spite of this manifestation ... the mystery of Jesus has remained hidden ... In whatever way he is understood, he remains utterly mysterious' (*Dionysius the Areopagite*). Inevitably this pervasive concept of the mystery of Christ spreads over into the eucharistic thinking about what Gregory of Nyssa terms 'the mystery given to the apostles' in which 'we are entitled to believe that the bread hallowed by the Word of God is transformed to become the body of the Word'.

The sacramental realism of the Fathers is subtle and we read of a spiritual body, a life-giving body and we meet terms like 'transfigured', 'transformed', a point that Jeremy Taylor, John Bramhall and Daniel Waterland were each quick to note. Constantly, the Johannine 'living bread' recurs and always it is, as Cyril of Jerusalem puts it, 'the Holy Spirit who sanctifies and transforms'. The Eucharist is for the new life, the rebirth of the individual believer within the Church, the temple of the Spirit. To become truly or fully human meant for the Fathers that process of restoring the image of God in which man was made and through grace reaches forward to his likeness: 'By the baptism of regeneration grace confers two benefits on us ... It gives the first immediately, for in the water itself it renews us, and causes the image of God to shine in us ... As for the other, it awaits our collaboration to produce it: it is the likeness of God' (*Diadochus of Photike*). As Irenaeus wrote, 'The Son of God was made man so that man might become son of God'. What these early Christian theologians are doing here is developing and emphasising that other Scriptural theme which is really part of 'the mystery of Christ'. It is the theme, referred to more than once by Jeremy Taylor, of 'partakers of the divine nature' (2. Pet 1.4), 'partakers of Christ' (Heb. 2.14), 'partakers of the Holy Spirit' (Heb. 6.4). This is everywhere in the Fathers and is what some of them mean by 'deification' and 'the deified person'. Cyril of Alexandria wrote that 'Participation in the Holy Spirit gives human beings the grace to be shaped as a complete copy of the divine nature'. This is the thinking which lies deep underneath the faith-encounter which takes place in the action of the Eucharist. This is why Taylor in his eucharistic writings reiterates for the communicant 'I live, yet not I, but Christ lives in me' and 'Christ who is our life': 'by the elements we live a new life in the Spirit and Christ is our bread and our life' (*The Worthy Communicant*, I(3)).

It is minds like these that have profoundly influenced leading Anglicans such as Lancelot Andrewes, Jeremy Taylor, William Forbes, James Ussher, Henry Hammond, William Wake, Herbert Thorndike and many others. With one accord they would have underwritten the passage from a sermon in which Andrewes had declared theological priorities: 'This Book chiefly, but in good part also, by the books of the ancient Fathers and lights of the Church, in whom the scent of this ointment was fresh'. Olivier Clément's outstandingly valuable work is not only a vivid illumination of the mind of the Fathers of the undivided Church for today's Christian. In respect of the theme of this book, it is in consequence, if indirectly, an illumination for the modern Anglican of one of the major sources of influence which helped to mould the thought of those whose understanding of the mystery of Christ and the mystery of the Eucharist we shall be examining. Moreover, when Clément writes that 'Tradition is not a written text ... it is the expression of the Spirit *juvenescens* ...

It is of course our foundation history, but it is also a living force', then there at once comes to mind the essential nature of the Anglican appeal to antiquity.

This element in the threefold appeal to Scripture, tradition and reason is both faith-guarding and identity-affirming. Tradition is the living Church interpreting 'the faith once for all delivered' (*Jude 3*) in the idom of each generation. The appeal to antiquity for Anglicans is primarily geared to affirming the present Church's identity with the Primitive Church in terms of a living continuity of faith and order. This is everywhere in the theology of the period. We meet it for example in that first essay in Anglican self-understanding, John Jewel's *Apology of the Church of England* (1562): 'We have returned to the Apostles and old Catholic fathers. We have planted no new religion but only have preserved the old that was undoubtedly founded and used by the Apostles of Christ and other holy Fathers of the Primitive Church'. Like Andrewes and Hammond, John Bramhall saw the visible Church as the actual continuation and embodiment of antiquity. This continuity of faith and order is the transmission of ecclesial life and saving truth: 'our religion is the same it was, our Church the same it was, our Holy Orders the same they were in substance'. The simple fact is that seventeenth-century Anglican theologians were steeped in the Fathers and their works. As Simon Patrick (1626–1707) would put it, their concern was not 'to run up a pedigree' but to affirm a continuity in that living force which in every generation proclaims through the Spirit 'the mystery of Christ' revealing the Father as love. In book after book, Jeremy Taylor (to give but one instance) demonstrates not only the very great extent of his patristic knowledge but how deeply immersed he is in the thought of the Fathers. From within the mystery he reflects on the mystery.

Those familiar with the range of Jeremy Taylor's eucharistic writings will endorse T. K. Carroll's comment that 'Taylor's eucharistic theology opened up from the patristic past a new or renewed way of understanding the Mystery that is ever ancient and ever new'.[6]

To enable people to reach on the concept of mystery, if that is not a contradiction in terms, and to relate it to Christian life and living, what he called 'making religion our business',[7] is Taylor's objective and one in which we may share by looking at several concepts as these were handled in the Anglican tradition yesterday and today.

II

Mystery, Materials and Grace

What happens at Holy Communion? Christ gives himself sacramentally in the body and blood of his paschal sacrifice and when this offering is met by faith, a life-giving encounter results. His real presence, effectually signified by the bread and wine is the mystery of the eucharist and at the heart of the action is the imparting of the life of Christ, crucified, risen and glorified, to the faithful communicant. So the Revised Catechism of the Church of Ireland reads: 'Receiving the Body and Blood of Christ means receiving the life of Christ himself, who was crucified and rose again, and is now alive for evermore'. What this is saying is that this real presence is a dynamic presence which finds 'its fulfilment in the unity of the body of Christ and in the sanctification of the believer'.[8] Richard Hooker had said the same: 'They which by baptism have laid the foundation and attained the first beginning of a new life have here their nourishment and food prescribed for continuance of life in them'.[9] Succinctly, Taylor notes 'by these it is that we have and preserve life', and again 'by them we live in a new life in the spirit, and Christ is our bread and our life'.[10] Christ present means Christ active. We are talking of 'presence' in personalist terms.

Into the understanding of the eucharistic action there enter as well as the concept of mystery, that of sacramentality and of the instrumentality of the elements as effectual signs conveying what they signify and the context of the eucharist is, as Lancelot Andrewes (1555–1626) stressed, the whole range and development of the Christian life. The master-theme for Jeremy Taylor is that of the *kainē ktisis*, the new life which is nourished by the word and sacrament: 'a new heart is put

11

into us, we serve under a new head, instantly we have a new name given us, and we are esteemed a new creation; and not only changed in manners, but we have a new nature within us ... this may seem strange, and indeed it is so, and it is one of *the great mysteriousnesses of the Gospel*'.[11] The life-transmitting grace of the sacrament is beautifully expressed by him in *The Worthy Communicant* (1660): 'He is the bread which came down from heaven; the bread which was born at Bethlehem; the house of bread was given us to be the food of our souls for ever. The meaning of which *mysterious and sacramental* expressions, when they are reduced to easy and intelligible significations, is plainly this: by Christ we live and move and have our spiritual being in the life of grace ... He took our life that we might partake of his; he gave his life for us, that he might give life to us'.[12]

This passage makes it clear that the concept of sacramentality cannot be separated from mystery, unexplained reality. Herbert Thorndike (1598–1672), an older contemporary of Taylor, put it like this: 'The fathers acknowledge the elements to be changed, translated, and turned into the substance of Christ's Body and Blood; though *as in a sacrament, that is, mystically*; yet, therefore, by virtue of the consecration, not of his faith that receives' and again 'If a man demand further, how I understand the Body and Blood of Christ to be present 'in', 'with', or 'under', the elements, when I say they are 'in', and 'with', and 'under', a *sacrament mystically*; I conceive I am excused of any further answer, and am not obliged to declare the manner of that which must be mystical'.[13] The same line of thought runs through all of Taylor's writings: 'So we may in this mystery to them that curiously ask, what, or how it is? 'Mysterium est'; 'It is a sacrament, and a mystery'; by sensible instruments it consigns spiritual graces'.[14]

It would be a serious misunderstanding to assume that for classical Anglicanism (or for that matter, patristic authors) the concept of mystery is an escape-clause. They were quite clear that sacraments are neither acted parables, the visual aids of grace, nor are they magic: 'For there is nothing ritual' says Taylor expounding sacramentality 'but it is also joined with something moral'. They are part and parcel of the religion of the Incarnation. The elements are expressive of the incarnational principle. The principle of a sacrament is that 'by the creatures it brings us to God; by the body it ministers to the spirit'.[15] The Anglicans believed that this was how it was meant to be since Scripture simply proclaims the gift of the Eucharist but reveals nothing of the manner How. Thus Lancelot Andrewes, who died in 1626, had written as early as 1610 in his *Responsio* to Cardinal Bellarmine: 'Christ said 'This is my Body'. He did not say, 'This is my Body in this way'. We are in agreement with you as to the end; the whole controversy is as to the method ... and because there is no word, we rightly make it not of faith ... we believe no less than you that the presence is real. Concerning the method of the presence, we define nothing rashly'.[16]

Forty years later, John Bramhall (1594–1663) of Armagh would affirm 'A true Real Presence; which no genuine son of the Church of England did ever deny ... Christ said *This is my Body*; what He said, we do steadfastly believe. He said not, after this or that manner, *neque con, neque sub, neque trans*. And therefore we place it among the opinions of the schools, not among the Articles of our Faith. The Holy Eucharist, which is the Sacrament of peace and unity, ought not to be made the matter of strife and contention'.[17] Taylor, conse-crated to the episcopate by Bramhall in 1661, summed it up neatly that there was no controversy 'till the manner became an article'. To exclude mystery is to go beyond Scripture and to evacuate sacramentality of all meaning: 'St Paul calls it "bread" even after consecration (1 Cor. 10.16) ... by Divine faith, we are taught to express our belief in *this mystery* in these words: The bread when it is consecrated and *made sacramental*, is the body of our Lord; and the fraction and distribution of it is the communication of that body, which died for us upon the cross'.[18] This, says Taylor, is what is meant by the Catechism of the Book of Common Prayer when it defines the sacrament of the Lord's Supper in which 'the thing signified' is 'the Body and Blood of Christ, which are verily and indeed taken and received' and taken 'after a heavenly and spiritual manner', the mean being faith: 'Verily and indeed' is 'reipsa', that is, 'really enough'; that is our sense of the real presence'.[19]

These three questions on the eucharist in the Catechism have been attributed to John Overall (1560–1619), bishop of Norwich, who wrote in his *Praelectiones* that 'In the Sacrament of the Eucharist or the Lord's Supper the body and blood of Christ, and therefore the whole Christ, are indeed really present, and are really received by us, and are really united to the sacramental signs which not only signify but also convey ... and therefore the whole Christ is communicated in the Communion of the Sacrament. Yet ... in a way *mystical*, heavenly, and spiritual, as is rightly laid down in our Articles'. Clearly, Overall, esteemed by John Cosin as 'his greatest teacher', considered this a fair outline of Anglican teaching and Jeremy Taylor offered a similar exposition in *The Real Presence and Spiritual* (1654): 'The doctrine of the Church of England and generally of the Protestants, in this article, is – that after the minister of the *holy mysteries* hath rightly prayed, and blessed or consecrated the bread and wine, the *symbols become changed* into the body and blood of Christ, after a *sacramental, that is, in a spiritual real manner*: so that all that worthily communicate, do by faith receive Christ really, effectually, to all the purposes of his passion ... the result of which doctrine is this: It is bread, and it is Christ's body. *It is bread in substance, Christ in the sacrament*; and Christ is really given to all that are truly disposed, as the symbols are; each as they can; Christ as Christ can be given; the bread and wine as they can ... *the first substance is changed by grace, but remains the same in nature*'.[20] Quite unequivocally and constantly he affirms a change in the eucharistic elements which is not physical or corporal: 'We say the conversion is figurative, *mysterious, and sacramental*'. Phrases such as 'change in condition', 'that great mysteriousness which is the sacramental change', 'the conversion', 'the symbols are changed into Christ's body and blood', recur throughout Taylor's writings. Yet in his language of change in the elements in a context of mystery and sacramentality he was not saying anything that other Anglicans before and after him were saying. Ridley had long before affirmed 'such a *sacramental mutation* I grant to be in the bread and wine, which truly is no small change, but such a change as no mortal man can make, but only the omnipotency of Christ's word ... the bread ceaseth not to be bread'.[21] For that matter, Cranmer himself had spoken of 'a sacramental conversion of bread and wine and of a spiritual eating and drinking of the body and blood' and insisted that 'Christ's flesh and blood be in the Sacrament truly present, but spiritually and sacramentally'.[22] So had Lancelot Andrewes and in the same terms: 'We allow that the elements are changed. But a change of substance we look for, and we find it nowhere' and again 'At the coming of the almighty power of the Word, *the nature is changed* so that what before was the mere element now becomes a *divine Sacrament*, the substance nevertheless remaining what it was before'.[23] In his *Preces Privatae*, used in successive generations since its posthumous publication in 1648, the themes of the new life and the mutual indwelling, the unity in the body and the sanctification of the believer, are enveloped in the mystery of the eucharistic action:

> So me too the ruined, wretched, and excessive sinner,
> deign to receive to the touch and partaking
> of the immaculate, supernatural, life-giving,
> and saving mysteries
> of Thy all-holy Body
> and Thy precious Blood.
> and come to sanctify us.
> O Thou who sittest on high with the Father,
> and art present with us here invisibly;

come Thou to sanctify the gifts which lie before Thee,
and those in whose behalf, and by whom,
and the things for which,
they are brought near Thee.
And grant us communion
unto faith, without shame,
love without dissimulation,
fulfilment of Thy commandments,
alacrity for every spiritual fruit.
We then remembering, O Sovereign Lord,
in the presence of Thy holy mysteries,
the salutary passion of Thy Christ,
that we, receiving in the pure testimony of our conscience,
our portion of Thy sacred things,
may be made one with the holy Body and Blood
    of Thy Christ;
and receiving them not unworthily,
we may hold Christ indwelling in our hearts,
and may become a temple of Thy holy Spirit
    Yea, O our God,
nor make any of us guilty
of Thy dreadful and heavenly mysteries
    nor infirm in soul or body
from partaking of them unworthily.

'The mystery of Thy dispensation ... is finished and done' he writes 'and we have been filled with Thy endless life'. The same three themes are seen in the prayer at the end of *Discourse XIX* in Taylor's *The Great Exemplar*: 'Let me for ever receive thee spiritually, and very frequently communicate with thee sacramentally, and imitate thy virtues piously and strictly ... let that holy sacrament of the eucharist be to me ... a means of sanctification and spiritual growth; that I receiving the body of my dearest Lord, may be one with his mystical body'.

What Andrewes expressed in devotional terms which are essentially poetry, his younger contemporary Richard Montague (1577–1641), bishop of Norwich, put with theological crispness in a book with the engaging title *A new Gag for an old Goose* (1624). There is no question, he says, but that the Church of England asserts 'the point of real presence' the only disagreement being the manner of the presence. 'Be contented with *That it is*, and do not seek nor define *How it is so*. Change, alteration, transmutation, and transelementation are not to be denied, and 'no man otherwise believeth but that the natural condition of the bread consecrated is otherwise than it was; being disposed and used to that holy use of imparting Christ unto the communicants'.[24] It bears on the relation of mystery to sacramentality to recall that Jeremy Taylor too went back to patristic sources in support of the real, spiritual presence: 'When the fathers, in this question, speak of the change of the symbols in the holy sacrament, they sometimes use the words ... "conversion, mutation, transition, migration, transfiguration", and the like ... but by these they do understand *accidental and sacramental conversions*, not proper, natural, and substantial'.[25] Nor should the use of two of these terms by Cranmer and Ridley be forgotten.

William Laud (1573–1645) of Canterbury, somewhat underrated as a theologian, edited the sermons of Andrewes and not surprisingly affirms the reality of the presence in the context of mystery. William Forbes (1585–1634) of Aberdeen, one of the 'Aberdeen Doctors', was also an admirer of Andrewes and inevitably one who looked to the early Fathers who, in Kenneth Stevenson's comment, 'are freer with their realist language but avoid the precision (over-precisions for him?) of the later medieval period'. His teaching marches with that of the better-known figures we have been considering.[26] Among these is, John Cosin (1594–1672), sequestered and exiled under the Commonwealth and made Bishop of Durham at the Restoration. Liturgist and author of *A Collection of Private Devotions* (1627) widely used and also attacked by Puritans, Cosin was a friend of Montague, whose book he defended and he produced several works on the theology of the eucharist. While Dugmore is, I believe, correct in detecting a subtle change in Cosin's views the bottom-line for him remains 'that in the Eucharist by virtue of the words and blessing of Christ the bread is *wholly changed in condition, use, and office*: that is, of ordinary and common, it becomes our *mystical and sacramental food*'. We are speaking of Christ's 'sacramental, spiritual, true and real Presence' and Cosin is at pains to show that the Fathers used and understood realist terminology in a mystic and spiritual sense.[27]

John Bramhall's life-story resembles the best type of fiction in which high office was replaced by penurious exile on the Continent because, as he wrote, he 'would not serve the times'. A marked man once the political storm had broken, he had two narrow escapes from being caught. His biographer, Vesey, recalled that Cromwell was reported to have said that 'he would have given a good sum of money for that Irish Canterbury'. During the tardy years of exile in conditions of poverty, Bramhall wrote seven works between 1649 and 1658 and in them his informed and solid Anglicanism, his knowledge of patristic and scholastic theology, are clear to the reader. The man who, as subdean at Ripon, had refused to leave his flock 'in a time of most contagious and destructive pestilence' was the same man who, as a proscribed exile, defended his persecuted church with an able pen. Man of affairs and theologian the story fittingly ends when in old age he was to consecrate twelve bishops in St Patrick's Cathedral, Dublin, in 1661 when Jeremy Taylor was the preacher, thus virtually reconstituting the sorely depleted Irish episcopate. As we have seen he held firm views on the eucharist in which 'the true, real presence' is seen in terms of mystery and sacramental efficaciousness. The manner of Christ's presence 'is incomprehensible to human reason' and 'can neither be perceived by sense, nor by imagination'. We are to 'rest in the words of Christ, 'This is my body' – leaving the manner to Him that made the Sacrament. We know it is sacramental and therefore efficacious'. The presence of Christ is sacramental, and therefore conveys what it signifies but as to how this is so 'we determine not'.[28]

Numerous other examples could be adduced but enough has been said to demonstrate the conviction of these theologians that as Taylor put it the first thousand years and Durandus were on the right track and he quotes the latter, 'We hear the word, we perceive the motion, we know not the manner, but we believe the presence'. Quite deliberately, Taylor (and here he speaks for the Others) insists that the strength of the doctrine of the real, spiritual presence is that mystery is at its heart: 'The presence of Christ is real and spiritual; *because this account does still leave the article in his deepest mystery*'.[29] Far from the intellectual bankruptcy of taking refuge in the idea of mystery, these men were asserting and affirming mystery as something irreducible in itself and the essential reality pervading the sacramental action and its effects – *the mystery of the Eucharist*.

With subtlety and in a manner strikingly consistent with the Resurrection narratives Taylor faces squarely 'what from early times underlies the expressions of sacramental realism and the various theories of change in or transmutation of the elements, namely, the nature of Christ's Body present in the Sacrament. *Was it the body born of Mary or not?* It is the question variously dealt with by Ratramn, Radbert and Berengar, subsequently reappearing in the sixteenth century, and answered from one side by the doctrine of transubstantiation, the concept of a change of substance. Taylor's solution is both simple and subtle: 'It is much insisted upon, that it be inquired whether when we say we believe Christ's body to be "really" in the sacrament, we mean "that body, that flesh, that was born of the Virgin Mary", that was crucified, dead, and buried?' He instances some of the Fathers, such as Jerome and Clement of Alexandria who reply in the negative but 'the meaning is easy: they intend that it is not eaten in a natural sense'. Thus their term a spiritual body is an affirmation of the manner not a distinguishing of one kind of body from another. The reality, says Taylor, is that the physical and the risen and glorified body of Christ is one, but differently apprehended. To the question he replies 'I know none else that he had, or hath: there is but one body of Christ natural and glorified: but he that says, that body is glorified, which was crucified, says it is the same body, but *not after the same manner*: *and so it is in the sacrament*; we eat and drink the body and blood of Christ, that was broken and poured forth; for there is no other body, no other blood of Christ: but though it is the same which we eat and drink, *yet it is in another manner*'.[30]

Jeremy Taylor is here affirming, to quote ARCIC I, that 'Christ is present and active in the eucharistic celebration ... and ... gives himself sacramentally in the body and blood of his paschal sacrifice ... and ... it is *the glorified Lord himself* whom the community of the faithful encounters in the eucharistic celebration'.[31] For Taylor this is a sacramental presence of Christ that is real and spiritual, personal and dynamic, and of very necessity this is 'the mystery of the eucharistic presence' in which 'we must recognize both the sacramental sign of Christ's presence and the personal relationship between Christ and the faithful which arises from that presence'.[32]

III

Parameters for the meaning of 'real'

The point which I have been endeavouring to make is that whether we are thinking of the eucharistic action and the elements in 'realist' terms (when an unspecified change in the elements is brought about by the Holy Spirit) or in 'dualist' terms (when the bread and wine are present with the body and blood) or even in terms of a qualified virtualism (as when Taylor says of the elements 'not only the sign and memorial of him that is absent, but it bears along with it the very body of the Lord, that is the efficacy and divine virtue of it)'[33] – we are essentially speaking of the *mystery* of the eucharist. Indeed, elements of all three approaches abound in Taylor's writings not because he could not make up his mind and plump for one school of thought but because he is deliberately resistant to classification. This richness of combined insights is remarkable only if we forget his intention, noted earlier, 'to gather together into a union all those several portions of truth, and differing apprehensions of mysteriousness'.

The whole theme of this Introduction to *The Worthy Communicant* is that of the mystery of the eucharist and of the proper preparation for it since 'the sacraments are mysteries, and to be handled by mystic persons'. What is involved for the communicant is that 'there is very much to be done on his part, there is a heap of duties, there is a state of excellency' and he may hope to receive 'the mysterious blessings' because 'the holy communion … is the most sacred, mysterious, and useful conjugation of secret and holy things and duties of religion'. Taylor analyses the different views there are of what happens at Holy Communion: 'some affirm the elements are to be blessed by prayers of the bishop or other minister;

21

others say, it is only by the mystical words, the words of institution: and when it is blessed, some believe it to be the natural body of Christ: others, to be nothing of that, but the blessings of Christ, his word and his Spirit, his passion in representment, and his grace in real exhibition: and *all these men* have something of *reason* for what they pretend; and yet the words of *Scripture* from whence they pretend are not so many as are the several pretensions'.

It is to be noted that Taylor is not saying that all are right and all have won the prize. Scripture and reason would appear to allow less probability to some views and indeed this is his thesis in *The Real Presence and Spiritual* where his criteria are Scripture, reason and sense. These, he maintains, protect the mystery by disallowing a presentation of it in terms of scientific and philosophical self-contradiction or seeing the eucharist as a mere memorial ceremony. The important thing is to look beyond the 'seemingly opposed doctrines, by which even good men stand at a distance, and are afraid of each other' to what lies behind them, 'some common truths, and universal notions, and mysterious and inexplicable words'. There 'it will not be impossible to find honey or wholesome dews upon all this variety of plants; and the differing opinions, and *several understandings of this mystery*, which (it may be) no human understanding can comprehend, will serve to excellent purposes of the Spirit'.

One wonders if today we have the clarity of vision and the intellectual courage to take a leaf out of Jeremy Taylor's book, seeing that theologians (and Churches) have in the past tied themselves in knots as they endeavour to explain the inexplicable, bequeathing the tangle and the divisions to those who come after,

> 'For last year's words belong to last year's language
> And next year's words await another voice'.

Taylor's last word in the Introduction is to declare 'the excellent mystery of the eucharist' and to relate it to what he calls 'the natural order of theology' in which faith and reason work together to produce the good life in which receiving the blessed sacrament is a major means of grace. The fact is that Taylor has learnt from Cambridge Platonists like his friend More (1614–1687) that reason is 'the breath of a higher divine reason'. It is 'the candle of the Lord'; it is *res illuminata illuminans*, so that Whichcote (1609–1683) could write, 'a man's reason is nowhere so much satisfied as in matters of faith'. For Taylor there is both a transcendental and an experiential element in reason. W. R. Inge's phrase about reason in the thought of the Cambridge Platonists comes to mind: 'an appeal to the inner experience of the whole man acting in harmony'. Reason's authority is mediated from God – 'It is the first participation from God' says Whichcote and to such a concept of reason mysticism (and mystery) are not foreign. Always for Taylor the sacrament remains 'this divine mystery' because 'there is one truth of the body in the mystery, and another truth simply and without mystery. It is truly Christ's body both in the sacrament, and out of it; but in the sacrament it is not the natural truth, but the spiritual and mystical'.[34]

IV

Mystery – And Reason?

If we follow Bunyan's *Pilgrim's Progress*, the function of theology is to be the Interpreter's House which has 'Significant
Rooms'.[35] When Taylor speaks, as he does, of 'several understandings of this mystery' and of 'reasons' for them we are
reminded that although the mystery of the Gospel is central
to his Christianity at the same time reason is a core-value in
his theology. In the *Ductor Dubitantium* (C.II, Rule III) he is
highly critical of those approaches to religion which only
'allow us to be Christians and disciples, if we will lay aside
our reason'. He shows none of the unease at coupling them
which we today experience, suggestible as we are to the contemporary implication that faith is believing what one knows
or suspects is not true. No doubt because of the influence on
his thinking which gives a warmth and an understanding of
reason as *lumen de lumine*, he does not seem to find any contradiction in linking mystery and reason: 'Into the greatest
mysteriousness of our religion, and the deepest articles of
faith, we enter by our reason: *not that we can prove every one
of them by natural reason*: for to say that, were as vain, as to
say that we ought to prove them by arithmetic or rules of
music; *but whosoever believes wisely and not by chance,
enters into his faith by the hand of reason*; that is, he hath
causes and reasons why he believes, indeed not wisely, but for
some reason or other he does it'.

Is this so very different from Austin Farrer's initial persuasion – 'the readiness to accept that "more" will be faith, or
the effect of faith'?[36] Jeremy Taylor's line is that faith includes
reason – 'reason lends legs to faith' – and continues on from
it, requiring an extra step: 'For it is to be considered, what-

soever is above our understanding, is not against it: *supra and secundum may consist together in several degrees*'. For him, reason leads us into such proportions of faith as it can. Faith demands the extra step because although our reason carries us to faith 'in many things she knows nothing but the face of the article' – 'we can see what, but not why; and what we do see, is the least part of that which does not appear'. What we cannot understand is not necessarily to be disbelieved. *In a true mystery, the more we understand the more we know there is more to understand.* There are mysteries of the Christian faith (he instances the function of the elements in the eucharist and of water in baptism) which are uncomprehended by us rather than incomprehensible, 'not to be comprehended by our dark and less instructed reason, but yet not impossible to believe'. In respect of these, 'our reason is not the positive measure of mysteries, and we must believe what we cannot understand'. Quite unequivocally Taylor says that because reason can only be 'a right judge when she is truly informed' here is where the obedience of faith comes in: 'the mysteries of faith are oftentimes like cherubim's heads placed over the propitiatory, where you may see a clear and bright face and golden wings, but there is no body to be handled; there is light and splendour upon the brow, but you may not grasp it; and though you see the revelation clear, and the article plain, yet the reason of it we cannot see at all; that is, the whole knowledge which we can have here, is dark and obscure … that is, we can see what but not why; and what we do see, is the least part of that which does not appear; but in these cases our understanding is to submit, and wholly to be obedient'.[37]

This digression into the relationship of faith and reason is designed to bring out Taylor's dual emphasis on reason and on mystery as two fundamental elements as he sees it in 'the natural order of theology'. It is not without significance for our subject here that the book which he considered his *magnum opus*, the *Ductor Dubitantium*, and in which he discusses this relationship was published in 1660, the same year in which *The Worthy Communicant* appeared. In the latter, he is 'posing the question, What specifically is the work and role of faith in the reception of Holy Communion? It cannot engage us to believe something contrary to our senses – Christ 'wrought faith in St Thomas by his fingers' ends'. This is true of the elements handled by priest and communicants which our senses tell us are bread and wine, but 'faith sees more in the sacrament than the eye does ... but nothing against it. Neither can faith oblige us to believe anything which is against right reason'. Here the substance of Taylor's eucharistic theology fits into the setting of his general theology and he reproduces the argument concerning faith and reason more fully developed in the *Ductor Dubitantium* ... Reason is not the positive measure of our faith and yet 'in all our creed there can be nothing against reason'. We must take care, however, that what we call reason is really reason and not something else. Reason is a right judge but it ought not to pass sentence in matters of faith 'until all the information be brought in'. Unless this is done, we 'may conclude well in logic, and yet infer a false proposition in theology'. Our experience and observation enter into the assessment as well as what is revealed. The 'natural' interpretation of the eucharistic presence cannot pass these tests ... and he returns to the familiar emphasis on mystery ... 'He hath hold us, This is his body, This is his blood: believe it, and so receive it: but he hath not told us how it is so'. The relation of faith to the elements is controlled, so to speak, by the fact that 'they are sacramental'. In other words, there is a real, spiritual presence, to be apprehended by faith, not created in it: 'The change is made by grace'; 'It remains after consecration the same it did before, but it is changed *inwardly* by the powerful virtue of the Holy Spirit'; 'by sensible things, he gives us insensible or spiritual'.[38]

So, towards the end of his life Taylor builds his exposition of the action and effects of the eucharist on the same two concepts, mystery and sacramentality.

We may well feel that in his evaluation of the faith/reason relationship Taylor would be regarded today as being over-optimistic in his conclusions, though how much of that judgment would be based on a concept of reason not identical with that held by Taylor is perhaps open to question. For him 'there is a *ragione di stato*, and a *ragione di regno*, and a *ragione di cielo*, after which none but fools will inquire, and none but the humble shall ever find'. It is unreasonable 'to pry into the reason of the mystery ... and to disbelieve the thing ... and say it is not at all, because he does not understand the reason of it'. We do well also when assessing this to picture at the same time a climate of greater belief in which acceptance and questioning kept company more closely than in ours. Taylor had a readiness (not then so common) to say 'I do not know', 'Beyond this we can do no more'.[39] It is from his utter conviction of the reality of the mystery that there comes this integrity of not knowing, this freedom to say that this is beyond me. Nor does he make any bones about suspending judgment in certain circumstances: 'When reason and revelation seem to disagree ... if right or sufficient reason can persuade us that this is not a revelation, well and good ... and if we cannot quit our reason or satisfy it, let us carry ourselves with modesty, and confess the revelation, though with profession of our ignorance and unskilfulness to reconcile the two litigants'.[40]

We catch here echoes of his older contemporary John Hales (1584–1656) who at the Synod of Dort bade John Calvin goodnight: 'It shall well befit our Christian modesty to participate somewhat of the sceptic ... till the remainder of our knowledge be supplied'. For him, as for Taylor, theologians would be advised to deal in 'more maybes and peradventures'.[41] There is in mystery an element of unknowing which paradoxically liberates something in the human spirit, almost an element of what John Robinson called that 'agnosticism which releases' and we catch a reflection of this in Taylor's presentation of the mystery of the eucharist. Rooted in imagery which is of the earth and of basic human needs the eucharist transposes all into a higher key. As Hooker put it: 'In the eucharist ... we understand that the strength of our life begun in Christ is Christ, that his flesh is meat and his blood drink, not by surmised imagination but truly, even so truly that *through faith* we perceive in the body and blood *sacramentally presented* the very taste of eternal life, the grace of the sacrament is here as the food which we eat and drink'; 'This bread hath in it more than the substance which our eyes behold'.[42]

This last extract may well cause raised eyebrows among those who appear to hold that Hooker's eucharistic thinking is neatly encapsulated in that renowned sentence, 'The real presence of Christ's most blessed body and blood is not therefore to be sought for in the sacrament, but in the worthy receiver of the sacrament'. Indeed, not to give full weight to the receptionist emphasis in Hooker would be to misrepresent his theology. Yet to label him as a receptionist *pur sang* would equally be a misrepresentation and a simplistic reading of his thought. In fact, his concern is to draw together to one focal point the 'givenness' of the Gift and the faith which receives the Gift and that point is the personal relationship created through the sacrament between Christ and the faithful: 'In the Eucharist we so receive the gift of God, that we know by grace what the grace is which God giveth us, the degrees of our own increase in holiness and virtue ...'.

Hooker's nineteenth-century commentator, Bishop Francis Paget in his *Introduction to the Fifth Book* (1899) acutely put his finger on this aspect of Hooker's thinking on the mystery of the eucharist: 'On the ground of some passages in his argument he is claimed as supporting one side in the very controversy from which he urged men to refrain ... Those who know Hooker's ways and do him justice will not easily think him so careless or so disingenuous as to break the bounds which he was strenuously appealing to other men to keep'. (p. 176).

The plain fact is that we are incapable of getting inside Hooker's mind-set so long as we lose sight for a moment of his chosen vocation as a theologian. This was to reknit and reconnect the disjunction, growing from the sixteenth century onwards, which was splitting theology right down the middle in almost every department from doctrine to liturgy. Not for nothing did he come to be known as 'the judicious Hooker'. In our own day, both Olivier Loyer and A. M. Allchin have underlined the category of *conjunction* as a vital element in Hooker's thought. I would suggest that this is notably the case in respect of his writing on the eucharist in the Fifth Book (LXVII) of the *Ecclesiastical Polity*.

For Hooker the eucharist is pre-eminently 'so high a mystery', 'the holy mysteries', 'this mystical communion', 'these mysteries (which) do as nails fasten us to his very Cross'. Central to his understanding of what happens at Holy Communion is the affirmation that 'the new life' begun in baptism is in the eucharist nourished 'for continuance of life' so that 'the strength of our life begun in Christ is Christ'. There is 'a *real participation* of Christ and of life in his body and blood *by means of this sacrament*' and 'no side denieth but that the *soul of man* is the receptacle of Christ's presence'. I would suppose that there is a sense in which St Augustine's 'your mystery is laid on the Table of the Lord, your mystery you receive', is saying much what Hooker is saying here when he writes that 'there ensueth a kind of transubstantiation in us, a true change both of soul and body'. What is at issue is lives transformed by the Life transmitted in the eucharist for 'Christ is *personally* there present, yea present whole'. This is its purpose, it heals, sanctifies and enlightens, 'it truly conformeth us unto the image of Jesus Christ'. What happens in the lives of faithful communicants is at the heart of the mystery of the eucharist. Everywhere in the following century this deep concern both with the purpose and the practical effects of the sacrament can be felt, ranging as Taylor was to put it from mending our pace to being partakers of the Divine nature – all the workings of grace from the small daily reform to the stupendous and exceptional refashioning.

So what then has this great exponent of conjunction to say on the subject of the presence? He wishes that men would 'meditate in silence what we have by the sacrament, and less to dispute of the manner how?' The 'endless mazes' and the 'curious and intricate speculations' are unfruitful but behind them lies 'a general agreement concerning that which alone is material' a real participation in Christ 'by means of this sacrament'. This real participation is the vital core for Hooker. This, rather than any formulation of the mode of the presence, is what really matters and he spells it out, having first dismissed Zwinglianism which regards 'this sacrament but only as a shadow, destitute, empty and void of Christ'. Because for him the eucharist is mystery it is observable throughout the section that Hooker preserves a reverent agnosticism about the manner how, partly because nothing is said about it in Scripture but primarily because the essential in the eucharist is 'our participation in Christ'. Thus he writes 'The fruit of the Eucharist is the participation of the body and blood of Christ. There is no sentence of Holy Scripture which saith that we cannot by this sacrament be made partakers of his body and blood except they be first contained in the sacrament or the sacrament converted into them. "This is my body", and "This is my blood", being words of promise sith we all agree that by the sacrament Christ doth really and truly in us perform his promise, why do we vainly trouble ourselves with so fierce contentions whether by consubstantiation, or else by transubstantiation the sacrament itself be first possessed with Christ, or no? *A thing which no way can either further or hinder us howsoever it stand*, because our participation in Christ in this sacrament dependeth on the co-operation of his omnipotent power which *maketh it his body and blood to us, whether with change or without alteration of the element such as they imagine we need not greatly to care nor inquire*'. In other words, Hooker's view of the controversy is to shift the emphasis from the means to the end, the purpose of the sacrament. Yet he goes not side-step the issue, approaching it with eirenic openness: 'The question is yet driven to a narrower issue ... whether when the sacrament is administered, Christ be whole *within man only*, or else his body and blood be also externally seated in the very consecrated elements themselves?'

How does Hooker handle this antithetic setting out of the question? In the first place, the elements are instrumental: 'The bread and cup are his body and blood because they are causes instrumental upon receipt whereof the participation of his body and blood ensueth. For that which produceth any certain effect is not vainly or improperly said to be that very effect whereunto it tendeth ... the sacraments really exhibit'. This is worthy of note since some but not all exponents of receptionism regard the elements as tokens rather than channels. Not so for Hooker's concept of instrumentality and he quotes approvingly those Fathers who affirm that in the sacrament Christ is *personally* there present, writing in a very significant passage 'that Christ assisting this heavenly banquet with his personal and true presence doth by his own divine power add to the natural substance thereof supernatural efficacy, *which addition to the nature of those consecrated elements changeth them and maketh them that to us which otherwise they could not be*; that to us they are thereby *made such instruments as mystically yet truly, invisibly yet really*, work our communion or fellowship with the person of Jesus Christ as well as in that he is man as God, our participation also in the fruit, grace and efficacy of his body and blood, whereupon there ensueth a kind of transubstantiation in us, a true change both of soul and body'.

This is a revealing paragraph setting out 'a real presence and spiritual' through the instrumentality of the elements taken up and used by Christ who is himself the Presence. This is very far from the position later to be rejected by such as Thorndike and Taylor that faith creates the presence. Care has to be taken in any assessment of receptionism proper, disregarding for the large part allegations of subjectivism (though in certain contexts there may be some substance in this) and taking account of its assertion of an objective Gift in the sacrament which is nevertheless to be associated not so much with the elements as with the reception of them. Even greater care should be taken in linking receptionism proper with Hooker – and there *is* a link – for he is endeavouring to repair what he sees as the disjunction in theological formulations and stated positions concerning the Gift offered in the mystery of the eucharist and the faith which responds to and apprehends the Gift. The fact is that Hooker is not to be conveniently pigeonholed as he reaches back to the patristic era for the exposition of what happens at Holy Communion: 'In a word it appeareth not that of all the ancient Fathers of the Church any one did ever conceive or imagine other than only a mystical participation of Christ's both body and blood in the sacrament, neither are their speeches concerning the change of the elements themselves into the body and blood of Christ such, that a man can thereby in conscience assure himself it was their meaning to persuade the world either of a corporal consubstantiation of Christ *with those sanctified and blessed elements* before we receive them, or of the like transubstantiation of them into the body and blood of Christ. Which both to our mystical communion with Christ are *so unnecessary*, that the Fathers who plainly hold but this mystical communion cannot easily be thought to have meant *any other change of sacramental elements than that which the same spiritual communion did require them to hold*'.

What we have here is a conjunction of the stress on faithful reception and on the instrumentality of 'those sanctified and blessed elements' with 'Christ assisting this heavenly banquet with his personal and true presence' in the overall context of participation. Hooker goes on to delineate this interpretation by examining the words 'This is my body' in terms of consubstantiation, of transubstantiation, and as presented by 'the Sacramentaries'. He identifies with the last group who affirm: 'This hallowed food, through concurrence of divine power, is in verity and truth, unto faithful receivers, instrumentally a cause of that mystical participation, whereby as I make myself wholly theirs, so I give them in hand an actual possession of all such saving grace as my sacrificed body can yield, and as their souls do presently need, this is *to them* and *in them* my body'.

This interpretation, says Hooker, affirms nothing that all views do not approve as true, does not go beyond what Christ said and 'the Church hath always thought necessary' and agrees with 'the writings of all antiquity'. Its telling advantage over the other two interpretations is that it shows no contradiction of 'true principles of reason grounded upon experience, nature and sense'. This is vintage Hooker whose book gave a perennial quality to Anglicanism and who wrote 'Theology, what is it but the science of things divine? What science can be attained unto without the help of natural discourse and reason?' (E.P. III, viii, 11) For Hooker, reason as *lumen de lumine* follows Scripture and precedes tradition in the threefold criteria by which the truth of any doctrine is established.

Probably this is as near as we can get to Hooker's eucharistic beliefs but the picture would be incomplete if reference were not made to what one can only call his deliberate reserve concerning the elements themselves, a reserve which one feels is consistent with his view that the eucharist is essentially mystery. We recall the sentence with which we began: 'This bread hath in it more than the substance which our eyes behold' and the reverent not-knowing in 'What these elements are in themselves, it skilleth not, it is enough that to me which take them they are the body and blood of Christ'. In LXVII (1) he writes of 'The power of the ministry of God ... by blessing visible elements it maketh them invisible grace'. In the end, for Hooker, it is the worshipping experience which is paramount: 'Let it therefore be sufficient for me presenting myself at the Lord's table to know what there I receive from him ... why should any cogitation possess the mind of a faithful communicant but This, O my God, thou art true, O my soul, thou art happy'.

It is surely possible to discern a line of theological descent from Hooker to Ussher on the one hand in respect of the change of use in the elements and the concept of an entitlement transmitted. Equally on the other hand, a line could run from Hooker to Taylor, who called him 'the incomparable Mr Hooker', in respect of a presence that is real and spiritual. Perhaps this in itself is an indication to us today of the importance of keeping in balance those elements which in a graced conjunction constitute the mystery of the eucharist.

V

The Richness of the Mystery

Obviously there have been amongst the Anglicans of the classical period a range of variations of emphasis and different conceptualizations of what happens at Holy Communion. One could maintain, and rightly, that the eucharistic theology of James Ussher (1581–1656) of Armagh, of Hooker's friend Richard Field (1561–1616), of the moral theologian Joseph Hall (1574–1656), was not as rich and profound as that of Taylor and that they lay more emphasis (but not *much* more) on 'the sacred use' of the elements. Yet in each of them there is to be found the dual stress on mystery and sacramentality as the two concepts which convey the meaning of what is taking place in the eucharistic action.

Ussher, for example, insists on a real, a personalist presence: 'We do not here receive only the benefits that flow from Christ, but the very Body and Blood of Christ, that is, Christ Himself crucified'. This is from his sermon before the House of Commons in 1620 in which the eucharist is 'this mystery' and 'this sacred action' understood only when we understand sacramentality. So he proceeds to expound what a sacrament is, not 'a bare sign' but 'a means of conveying the same to us'. He spells this out: 'a sacrament, taken in its full extent, comprehendeth two things in it, – that which is outward and visible which the Schools call properly *sacramentum*, in a more strict acceptation of the word; and that which is inward and invisible, which they term *rem sacramenti*, the principal thing exhibited in the sacrament. Thus in the Lord's Supper the outward thing, which we see with our eyes, is bread and wine; the inward thing which we apprehend by faith is the Body and Blood of Christ. In the outward part of this *mystical action*, which reacheth to that which is *sacramentum* only, we receive this Body and Blood but *Sacramentally*; in the inward, that containeth *rem*, the thing itself in it, we receive them *really*. And consequently the presence of these in the one is *relative and symbolical*, in the other *real and substantial*'.

Use and consecration effect a change in the elements but Ussher does not, like Taylor, join change of condition with change of use: 'The Bread and Wine are not changed in substance' – Taylor and the Others emphatically concur – 'from being the same with that which is served at ordinary tables. But in respect of the sacred use whereunto they are consecrated, such a change is made that now they differ as much from common bread and wine, as heaven from earth. Neither are they to be accounted barely *significative*, but truly *exhibitive* also ... as being appointed by God to be a means of conveying the same unto us ... the Body and Blood of Christ. And this is *that real and substantial presence* which we affirmed to be in the inward part of this *sacred action*'.[43]

Hall taught a real spiritual presence emphasising, to quote C. W. Dugmore, that 'the elements remain bread and wine in respect of nature and essence, but they convey to the faithful receiver the body and blood of Christ in the spiritual use of them. It is the crucified not the glorious body of Christ which is received in the sacrament'.[44] Field, like all the others rejected what they variously termed a 'carnal', 'corporal', 'local' presence but held that the consecrated elements are the body of Christ 'in *mystery* and *exhibitive* signification'.[45] Field and Andrewes were contemporaries as was William Forbes on whose writings the influence of Andrewes is perceptible and indeed acknowledged. 'This presence' he writes 'is not natural, corporeal, carnal, in itself local, but without any departure from heaven and supernatural'. It is a real, personalist presence, 'the presence of Christ the Lord *in the Sacrament*, Who is present in a wonderful but real manner'. Sacrament and mystery are one: 'he who worthily receives *these mysteries* of the Body and Blood of Christ really and actually receives into himself the Body and Blood of Christ, but in a certain *spiritual, miraculous and imperceptible way*'. This is very like Andrewes and the stress on mystery continues as he writes 'the Body and Blood of Christ are really and actually and substantially present and taken in the Eucharist, but in a way which the human mind cannot understand and much more *beyond the power of men to express*, which is known to God alone and is not revealed to us in the Scriptures'. As I have been suggesting, Forbes sees mystery as a Divine secret not transparent to man but revealing its nature and origin by its effects. Like Taylor he underlines the central rôle of the Holy Spirit in the mystery of the eucharist: 'In the Supper by the wonderful power of the Holy Ghost we invisibly partake of the substance of the Body and Blood of Christ, of which we are made recipients no otherwise than if we visibly ate and drank his Flesh and Blood'.[46] Forbes was a patristic scholar and was aware of Eastern Orthodox beliefs and liturgy hence no doubt his stress on the place of the Spirit in the eucharistic action and both these points are also the case with Taylor whose eucharistic theology consciously looks back to the Fathers and whose liturgical experiments show the influence of the liturgies of St Basil, St James and St John Chrysostom.

We meet the same reference back to the Fathers and the same emphasis on the mystery of Christ's presence in *A Practical Catechism* (1664) by Henry Hammond. Ejected from his parish of Penshurst and imprisoned, he lived after his release in retirement during which his numerous works were widely influential in sustaining Anglican morale during the Commonwealth: 'It is certain that many of the ancient fathers of the Church conceived very high things of this Sacrament, acknowledged the bread and wine to be changed, and to become other than they were; but not so as to be transubstantiate into the body and blood of Christ, to depart from their own substance, or figure, or form, or to cease to be bread and wine *by that change*; and that the faithful do receive the body and blood of Christ in the Sacrament, which implies not any corporal presence of Christ on the table, or in the elements,but God's communicating the crucified Saviour, who is in heaven bodily, and nowhere else, to us sinners on earth, but this *mystically*, and after an ineffable manner. And generally *they make it a mystery*, but descend not to the revealing of the manner of it, leaving it as a matter of faith, but not of sense, to be believed, but not grossly fancied or described.'

Our survey has shown that in one form or another the mystery/sacramentality theme is central to the presentation of the action of the eucharist by a majority of Anglican theologians in the seventeenth century. This theology of 'the holy mysteries' and of the real spiritual presence of Christ with and through the elements which are not only effectual but instrumental has continued on to later times. Recently my attention was drawn[47] to *An Inquiry into Eucharistic Symbols* (Dublin 1824) by the Irish lay-theologian Alexander Knox, friend of Bishop Jebb of Limerick and of John Wesley and who has been regarded as a precursor of the Oxford Movement. I have no direct evidence that Taylor was studied by Knox though it is highly improbable given the latter's background and thinking, that he was not acquainted with Taylor's work. In any event, the influence of Taylor's type of eucharistic theology at least is clear. One bears in mind also Taylor's influence on Knox's friend John Wesley and on that leader of the Oxford Movement, John Keble, an influence specifically acknowledged by both. For the Tractarians William Palmer and John Keble and E. B. Pusey the eucharist is that 'high and holy mystery' in which through 'a real change ... effected by Consecration' Christ is present in a special way, 'a presence the manner of which is beyond all thought' – thus Palmer and Keble on what they termed 'a peculiar and personal presence'. Pusey adds that 'the term "in", as used by the fathers, does not express any "local" inclusion of the body and blood of Christ: *it denotes their presence after the manner of a Sacrament* ... The presence ... is in a supernatural, divine, ineffable way'. The more one reads John Keble and E. B. Pusey the more one recognizes that they are speaking the same language as their seventeenth-century predecessors. Indeed, in his *On Eucharistical Adoration*, Keble quotes extensively from many of them on the eucharistic presence. Taylor, Overall, Laud, Thorndike, Cosin and Nicholson are all cited and one recalls that Keble's edition of Hooker's *Works* (1836) was the first modern and critical edition. His wide knowledge and use of the Fathers is in the same Anglican tradition and as with the seventeenth-century theologians the appeal to antiquity is for him a vital and essential element in the classic threefold appeal to Scripture, tradition and reason: 'We stand as orthodox Catholics upon a constant virtual appeal to the oecumenical voice of the Church, expressed by the four great Councils, and by general consent in all the ages during which she continued undivided'. H. P. Liddon regarded *On Eucharistical Adoration* (1857) as 'one of the most beautiful of his contributions to the treasures of the Church of England' and the author himself considered it to be one of his most useful products. For Keble, 'the gift in the Holy Eucharist is Christ Himself – all good gifts in one'. The gift is in sacrament and mystery, 'in an immense, *inconceivable* degree', Christ 'coming by a peculiar presence of His own divine Person, to impart Himself to each one of us separately, coming with these unutterable *mysteries* of blessing, coming with His glorified Humanity'. Constantly he speaks, as does Alexander Knox, of 'a special mode of Presence', 'a peculiar and personal Presence' and always the stress is on the mystery of the Eucharist, 'a Presence the manner of which is beyond all thought, much more beyond all words of ours'. As to the elements, they are unchanged in their nature and are effectual instruments: 'the presence of that Bread and Wine is to us a sure token of the Presence of Christ's Body and Blood'. We no more worship the elements than the woman with the issue of blood thought to worship 'the garment she touched, instead of Him who was condescending to wear it and make it an instrument of blessing to her'. The sign conveys the thing signified 'by a spiritual and heavenly process'. He regards transubstantiation as being 'if not the origin, at least the main aggravation of all our present difficulties on the subject of Holy Communion'. He contrasts it with 'the Real Objective Presence' (one thinks of Taylor) which he finds when he comes to answer the question 'But what says Christian antiquity?' Examining the Fathers and Councils, Keble holds that he can find no evidence of belief in a change of nature and of substance and, interestingly, among his many references he cites the fifth century Theodoret as did Taylor before him and Will Spens after him: 'It is untrue that after consecration the mystical symbols depart out of their proper nature; remaining as they do in their former substance, and figure, and form, and being visible and tangible, just as they were before. But the inward sense perceives them as being simply what they have become, and so they are the object of faith, and are adored, as being those very things which they are believed to be'.

If we turn to Pusey's famous sermon preached before the University of Oxford in 1853, 'The Presence of Christ in the Holy Eucharist', we find the same theology of the eucharist. The paradox is that the key to the meaning and the reality of what happens at Holy Communion should be mystery and sacramentality. Yet, as we have already noted, that is exactly what Pusey is saying. Two years later he published *The Doctrine of the Real Presence in the Fathers*, a large volume which in effect was a series of notes with commentary in support of the sermon. The material is handled with a massive learning and an almost surgical precision. The main thrust is that, in the patristic writings, it can be shown that the Fathers affirming a real presence believed that the elements continued in their natural substance. They are not bare elements but are changed by the supernatural operation of the Holy Spirit, a change which is not physical but *sacramental*: 'the Eucharistic elements are an outward reality, figuring to us that hidden reality, which sacramentally they convey to us'. Like his predecessors, Taylor, Bramhall and Waterland, he discusses the patristic terms 'in, under, with, the bread and wine' and gives examples, concluding: 'The term "*in*" as used by the Fathers, does not express any "local" inclusion of the Body and Blood of Christ; it denotes their presence there after the manner of a Sacrament ... the Presence of our Lord's Body and Blood in the Holy Eucharist is in a supernatural, Divine, ineffable way, not subject to the laws of natural bodies. The word *in*, like the word of our Book of Homilies, "*under* the form of Bread and Wine", only expresses a real Presence under that outward veil. But the term *does* imply the existence of the elements, *in* which the Body and Blood of our Lord are said to be'. In the same way, Pusey examines the use by the Fathers of such terms as transelement, re-order, transform, transfigure, become, translate, concluding that they imply sacramental change only and not that 'the *substance* of the elements *ceases to be*'.

Pusey had conceived the idea of a 'Library of the Fathers' as early as 1836 and it became influential running to over forty volumes by 1885, the first of which, St Augustine's *Confessions*, was translated by Pusey himself who contributed prefaces to more than half a dozen others. If Lancelot Andrewes helped to strengthen and establish the appeal to antiquity as a norm in Anglican apologetic for the seventeenth century, Pusey performed a like service to the Church in his own day, believing as he did that the Fathers were gradually being forgotten as the eighteenth century advanced.

Contemporary with Keble and Pusey was Robert Isaac Wilberforce whose *Sermons on the Holy Communion* (1854) were set in the less rarefied atmosphere of the parish church and who insisted that the real presence is taught by the Prayer Book. First, like Knox, he concentrates on the symbols, the elements, and asserts 'that which we are considering is the function and efficacy of the bread and wine; and, again, that of the Body and Blood of Christ. Are the former only a sign by which we are reminded of the latter; or are they the medium of their presence?' Not wishing to dazzle his hearers with 'isms' Wilberforce outlines three 'systems which may be supposed to occupy the field' – in effect, Zwinglianism, transubstantiation and virtualism. How far, he asks, does the Church of England favour any of them? Most significantly for the theme of our book he observes 'If it be objected to any of them that it is a *mysterious* statement, this would be in its favour ... because our Church speaks twice over of this service as a *holy mystery*'. He then goes straight to the Catechism answer: 'The Catechism tells us that our Lord has commanded us to receive the outward part – bread and wine; but when it comes to the inward part, it affirms with great positiveness, that 'the Body and Blood of Christ are *verily* and *indeed taken* and *received* by the faithful in the Lord's Supper' (italics in text).

The fact is that, as we shall be noting, this Catechism answer and its companion always were and are a constant stabilizing point of reference in Anglican eucharistic thought. His conclusion then is: 'The Body and Blood of Christ, but not, of course, in any natural or carnal manner, is the thing present, which the elements convey; and there follows from it the spiritual power and virtue whereby our souls are strengthened. And hence ... comes that phrase of a *Real Presence*, the exact meaning of which is often mistaken ... a real presence means the presence of a *res* or thing; as distinguished either from the sign which represents, or the influence which emanates from it. And such is the kind of presence which the Catechism affirms'. Like the Carolines before him (and he quotes Hooker, Overall and others) Wilberforce is profoundly aware in these sermons that eucharist in mystery is contextualized by ethics and the practical: 'Let us conclude with a single word of a practical character. If such be the real nature of this holy rite, how deep should be the earnestness with which we should approach it … the true preparation is such a mode of life as may oppose no impediment to His entrance'. A whole sermon is devoted to the new creation, 'the re-creation in Christ' of men and women. Inseparable from this is the transcendence of the mystery of the Eucharist since 'it is by spiritual power and by the intervention of God the Holy Ghost, that our Lord's supernatural presence is imparted', for it is the same Spirit who also regenerates and recreates the members of the new household of faith: 'The Church is the preparation for heaven; the regenerate nature enjoys a foretaste here of its future portion; already is it sealed with that Holy Spirit of promise'. What happens through the Spirit in the mystery of the eucharist is that 'earthly elements receive that blessing, whereby they are made the medium of a heavenly gift … this supernatural presence of Christ is the work which is brought about through the words of consecration'. This too is the theological ambience of Knox's thinking.

Knox is at pains to emphasise that Christ is here 'specially present' and that 'a special presence' is pledged by the instrumental and effectual symbols in the eucharist.[48] This real and spiritual presence is dynamic and personal, 'quickening us with his divine vitality'.[49] He insists on 'the invisible mystery of the eucharist'[50] and, like Andrewes and Taylor, he sees the principle of sacramentality as naturally expressive of the religion of the Incarnation.[51] The eucharist therefore is 'not figurative, but mysterious and transcendental'.[52] It is not 'a mere commemorative and covenanting transaction'.[53]

The symbols are 'in virtue and efficacy, his body and blood' and they have a 'transcendent quality'[54] Knox makes his meaning even clearer when he speaks of 'the *mysterious* character and efficacy which the material elements of bread and wine acquired by their consecration to the holy purpose for which they are appointed'.[55] What happens in the eucharist is that 'by making the eucharistic elements to be effectually what he had named them', Christ is 'graciously and influentially present in those *holy mysteries*'.[56] He criticizes Waterland (1683–1740) specifically for excluding the concept of mystery from the elements[57] and further on he observes that whenever there is a 'rejecting the mysterious instrumentality of the symbols' the result is that 'the ordinance itself has appeared to lose its interest and attractiveness'.[58] We see here, of course, the identical emphasis Taylor makes in his constant references to a changed condition and a mysterious conversion. One can find another parallel with Taylor's combination of the concepts of a real spiritual presence and of virtue in Knox. He says 'a divinely effective virtue became, through consecration, *mysteriously united* with the eucharistic symbols' and 'the eucharistic elements ... are in an inexplicable but deeply awful manner, the receptacles of that heavenly virtue'.[59] He makes a plea for 'deep views of the Sacrament'[60] and we even find the anticipatory term 'value' which Brevint too used on one occasion: 'the same infinite value ... of the communion of the Lord's body and the Lord's blood'.[61]

There comes to mind that other Irish lay-theologian James Bonnell (1653–1699), the devout Accountant General of Ireland of whom his friend Bishop Wetenhall said 'I am truly of opinion that, in the best age of the Church on earth, had he lived therein, he would have passed for a saint'. His biographer knew him, drew upon their friends for written accounts, and had the use of Bonnell's 'own private papers ... what he himself calls them, the transcript of his heart'.[62] We are thus protected from that kind of hagiography in which distance lends enchantment. Bonnell's was the piety of Taylor's *Holy Living* and he early adopted a rule of life, going to church twice every day no matter how busy he was and keeping to a pattern of prayers in private at rising, washing and dressing – the pattern we meet in Taylor's *Golden Grove*. It was in fact, Bonnell himself tells us, Lewis Bayly's *The Practice of Piety* which early led him straight to what he calls 'the proposal of a methodical course of religion'. The personality that emerged was a civil servant of admired integrity, a man of moral and physical courage, one whose 'peculiar charms and graces almost ravished those that conversed with him' according to another friend William King. His biographer Hamilton presents him as 'an instance of one who reconciled a life of religion and business together'.[63] Bonnell, self-disciplined and humble, was approachable and attractive: 'none made greater allowance for human nature'.[64] His personal charities, 'always managed with the greatest secrecy', were later computed by 'his intimate friends' to be 'the eighth part of his yearly income'.[65]

This is the man who at his weekly eucharist would shorten his devotions so as not to be noticeable when put in a front seat and who, on his return home, composed for his own instruction eucharistic meditations. As with Taylor the true context of the Holy Sacrament is holy living, the transforming of the Christian's daily experience by the life-changing mystery: 'My Saviour *impregnated the consecrated elements* and *in a manner embodied himself there*; yet still remaining where he was, filling heaven and earth but more particularly our chancel: saying to us: You are all my friends and worthy, whatever your sins be, through my sufferings'. Here we have the familiar 'holy mystery' of the eucharist and Bonnell shows us the elements as 'these holy mysteries' when he writes: 'The Holy Elements are impregnated with the materials of life, like the first framing of a living creature or embryo before it is quickened. But they are quickened with spiritual life only upon the faith of each receiver which God hath appointed to be the *concurring instrument* or means of this divine quickening'. The presence is given and real, Christ has 'impregnated the consecrated elements' and has 'embodied himself there' through the Spirit. Faith does not create Christ's presence but faith as a 'concurring instrument' apprehends and appropriates it. The presence and the faith are both the Spirit's work and are inseparable in what happens at Holy Communion. The eucharist is 'immortal love wrapt up in bread' and the 'glorious bread' and the communicant's faith concur in the renewal and transformation of daily experience into that new life which is the goal of Christian believing and behaving.[66]

VI

Mystery, Morality and Practicality

Here is paradox, that the mystery issues demandingly in the moral and the practical. If we needed a text for this section Taylor provides it in the concluding paragraphs, already referred to, of the introduction to *The Worthy Communicant* in the dedication of which 'the eucharist is, by the venerable fathers of the church, called the queen of mysteries'.

His declared purpose is to set out the nature and purpose of the sacrament and 'all the duties of preparation', in order 'that we may understand what it is that we go about'. Always, for him, mind keeps company with mystery harmonically and morals essentially flow from this conjunction. Already he has laid it down that the inevitable context of eucharistic theology is moral/ascetic theology. This was in his first major work *The Great Exemplar* (1649) in which he wrote that 'there is nothing ritual, but it is also joined with something *moral*, and required, on our part, in all persons capable of the use of *reason* ... the external rite of sacrament is so instrumental in a spiritual grace, that it never does it but with the conjunction of something moral'.[67] The mystery is both sacrifice and sacrament and the consequence of faithful reception is new life in Christ: 'For, as it is a commemoration and representment of Christ's death, so it is a commemorative sacrifice: as we receive the *symbols and the mystery*, so it is a sacrament. In both capacities, the benefit is next to infinite ... For whatsoever was offered in the sacrifice, is given in the sacrament ... and every holy soul having feasted at his table, may say, as St Paul, 'I live yet not I, but Christ liveth in me'. So that 'to live is Christ': 'Christ is our life'.[68] In other words, practical divinity and eucharistic theology are inseparably meshed together in the mystery of the eucharist, for 'holy living' is a consequence of 'holy communion' and 'holy communion' is a gracious aid in 'holy living': 'We must bring faith along with us, and God will increase our faith; we must come with charity, and we shall go away with more'.

Now, in one of his latest works *The Worthy Communicant* (1660) he underlines this essential merging of mystery, morality and religious practice in almost definitional form: 'Every time we receive the holy sacrament, all our duties are summed up; we make new vows, we chastise our negligence, we mend our pace, we actuate our holy purposes, and make them stronger; we enter upon religion, as if we had never done anything before'.[69]

This is the core of Taylor's book and the final paragraph of the introduction not only sets out our theme but uncovers the foundations of Caroline eucharistic thinking and teaching and practice: 'It matters not where we begin; for if I describe the excellencies of this sacrament, I find it engages us upon matters of duty, and inquiries practical: if I describe our duty, it plainly signifies the greatness and excellency of the mystery: the very notion is practical, and the practice is information; we cannot discourse of the secret, but by describing our duty; and we cannot draw all the lines of duty, but so much duty must needs open a cabinet of mysteries'.

Our right reason leads us to look on the mystery and the mystery leads into the good life: 'If we understand what we are about, we cannot choose but be invested with fear and reverence; and if we look in with fear and reverence, it cannot be but we shall understand many secrets. But because the natural order of theology is by faith to build up good life, by a rectified understanding to regulate the will and the affections, I shall use no other method, but *first discourse of the excellent mystery*, and then of the duty of the communicant, direct and collateral'.[70]

The elements, says Taylor, 'are made to be signs of a secret mystery ... instruments of grace ... and by these the Holy

Spirit changes our hearts and translates us into a divine nature'.[71] Christ present in the eucharist is present in a manner 'never to be drawn nearer than a mystery, till it comes to experience, and spiritual relish and perception'.[72] What happens at Holy Communion is that 'the Spirit blesses the symbols, and assists the duty' so that the whole man and the eucharistic action are taken up into His operation: 'Neither the outward nor the inward part does effect it, neither the sacrament nor the moral disposition; only the Spirit operates by the sacrament, and the communicant receives it by his moral dispositions, by the hand of faith'.[73]

Thus does Taylor set the scene to show how the fruit of the mystery is morality, the practice of the good life and how the obedience of a Christian man in turn illuminates the mystery which is 'Christ in you, the hope of glory': 'He that desires to enter furthest into the secrets of this mystery ... can better learn by love than by inquiry'.[74]

Much the greater part of *The Worthy Communicant* is therefore devoted to the remote and to the immediate preparation in order to 'the participation of the mysteries'. Structured on an analysis of faith, charity and repentance as 'preparatory to the blessed sacrament' it discusses self-examination and provides 'acts of virtues and graces relative to the Mystery'. The length of the book is in part redeemed by the profundity of its insights into the human psyche and by its treatment of the subject showing the obvious skill of the author in spiritual direction and counselling.

The five preparative chapters illustrate how Jeremy Taylor locates his theology of the eucharist solidly within a restructured moral theology (of which he was a leading exponent) and the distinctive spirituality which flows from it. This he had already demonstrated in *The Great Exemplar* and in *Holy Living* for always he sees the moral and the practical – our forbears dubbed the subject 'practick divinity' – flowing from the mystery, for Christ is 'present to us, not in mystery only, but in blessing also'.[75] So, 'our general preparation ...

to the participation of the mysteries ... is a relative duty, and is not for itself, but for *something beyond* ... there is no duty in Christianity, that is partly solemn and partly moral, that hath in it more solemnity and more morality than this one duty ... when they come to receive this holy sacrament'.[76]

The purpose of his book then is to promote a real self-examination which produces real results. We must 'betake ourselves to the solid and material practices of a religious life'.[77] *In a sense, that says it all* and this is what informs Taylor's analysis of the relation of faith, love and repentance to the mystery of the eucharist, to what happens in Holy Communion and to what happens to the faithful communicant as he participates in Holy Communion: 'the bread indeed is our food, but the virtue which is in it, is that which gives us life; by faith and efficacy, by hope and *the perfection of the mysteries*, and by the title of sanctification, it should be made to us the perfection of salvation'.[78]

Here one is irresistibly reminded of the impact of the major Anglican reform, the fusing in one instrument of moral and ascetical theology long treated as separate subjects – a reform anticipating the whole trend of moral theology in our own day. The objective of the science was no longer to deal for the most part in classifying sins and setting repentance in the framework of *poenitentia*. The subject was not so much the penitent at the tribunal as the Christian in the Church. The Anglicans were aiming at producing one integrated science of moral-ascetical theology, the art of full co-operation with grace in a total Christian life. Thus Taylor would describe moral theology as 'the life of Christianity' and 'the life of religion'[79] and Robert Sanderson, the doyen of Anglican moral theologians, had provided a trend-setting definition in one of his sermons to the clergy: 'But when all is done, positive and practique Divinity is it must bring us to Heaven: that is, it must poise our judgements, settle our consciences, increase our graces, strengthen our comforts, save our souls ... There is no study to this, none so well worth the labour as

this, none that can bring so much profit to others, nor therefore so much glory to God, nor therefore so much comfort to
our own hearts as this'.[80] This is the kind of moral theology
which runs through Taylor's books and sermons. In his own
words it is aimed 'towards the sanctification of the whole
man'. It focuses on the imitation of Christ into whom the
Christian has been incorporated through baptism. Its goal is
'the new life', 'the new creature', 'the new possibility', to use
favourite terms of his, and it is a moral theology accordingly
oriented to growth, centred on Christian maturation. It
thinks in terms of *metanoia* rather than *poenitentia* and it
speaks the language of the Kingdom rather than that of
jurisprudence. It is a moral theology sited in the *kerygma*,
being concerned with 'nature restored by the Gospel,
engaged to regular living by new revelations, and assisted by
the Spirit'. Its goal is 'walking in newness of life', in 'obedi-
ential faith'.[81] It is this approach to the Christian calling
which informs the preparative chapters of *The Worthy Communicant*. This is the basic understanding of religion which
colours Taylor's relating of the mystery of the eucharist to the
whole Christian practice, internal and external, to believing
and behaving. He has been speaking of the manner and
meaning of Christ's presence in 'these divine mysteries' and
he continues that two things follow: '1. That the divine mysteries are of very great efficacy and benefit to our souls. 2.
That faith is the great instrument in conveying these blessings
to us'.

Then, in a striking passage, he sets out in detail how the
mystery issues in the moral and the practical for the baptized
member of the eucharistic fellowship as he seeks through
grace to relate his obedience to his faith:

> But all the inquiry (i.e. into the nature of the presence) is not
> yet past: for thus we rightly understand the mysterious propo-
> sitions; but *thus* we *do not fully understand the mysterious
> sacrament*. For since coming to Christ in all the addresses of
> Christian religion, that is, in all the ministries of faith, – is eat-

ing of the body and drinking the blood of Christ, what does faith in the reception of the blessed sacrament that it does not do without it? ... here I am to add, that in *the holy communion all the graces of a Christian, all the mysteries of the religion are summed up* as in a divine compendium; and whatsoever moral or mysterious is done without, is, by a worthy communicant, done more excellently in this divine sacrament. *For here we continue the confession of our faith which we made in baptism*; here we perform in our own persons what then was undertaken for us by another; here that is made explicit, which was but implicit before; what then was in the root, is now come to a full ear; *what was at first done in mystery alone, is now done in mystery and moral actions, and virtuous excellencies together*; here we do not only hear the words of Christ, but we obey them ... For this is the chief of all the Christian mysteries, and the union of all the Christian blessings, and the investiture of all Christian rights, and the exhibition of the charter of all Christian promises, and the exercise of all Christian duties. *Here is the exercise of our faith, and acts of obedience, and the confirmation of our hope, and the increase of our charity* ... in the worthy reception of this divine sacrament, there must be a conjugation of virtues, and, therefore, we serve God more.

He concludes: 'That by "faith" in our dispositions and preparations to the holy communion, is not understood only "the act" of faith, but "the body" of faith, not only believing the articles, but the dedication of our persons; not only a yielding up of our understanding, but the engaging of our services; nor the hallowing of one faculty, *but the sanctification of the whole man*'.[82]

Here is how the mystery of the eucharist appears to one who is primarily a moral theologian and a preacher and spiritual director much sought after as a counsellor according to his friend George Rust, a practical theologian fond of affirming that we should 'make religion the business of our lives'. Taylor wants us to be 'transformed into a new nature' and instrumental in this process is what I have christened the Anglican spirituality of the five Ds, devotion, duty, discipline, detail and doctrine. This is everywhere in the devotional and

catechetical writings of the period, an exacting and disciplined devotion detailed in application with prayers at rising,
washing and dressing and always the goal is the new life in
Christ and lived in the situations of ordinary living. A typical
example is a book by the layman Robert Nelson. First published in 1698, it went into many editions during the following century. 'Solid and substantial piety' (Preface) is aimed at
in a religious programme including daily church attendance,
prayers for business and recreation, rising and bed-time,
meals and fasting. The means of grace have as their objective
'that we should become *new creatures* ... a man may be a bad
man, and use them all; and yet there is no being good without them'. 'The exact performance of duties' is essential for
'Christian perfection consists in the right performance of
such actions as ordinarily occur every day'. He analyses the
means of grace, especially the eucharist, and treats each
virtue in detail. The means are essential to the end, for virtue
'disposes to the beatific vision'.[83] The same pattern of spirituality runs through *Christian Consolations* (1671) by
Taylor's senior contemporary John Hacket, bishop of
Lichfield. It deals with faith, hope, the work of the Spirit,
prayer and the sacraments. It is a piety of discipline aimed at
the *kainē ktisis*: 'Keep strictly as much as you are able' to regular devotions; 'Offer up not only your prayers, but the strict
observation of set times' but 'prayers like little posies, may be
sent forth on every occasion'. The means and the end are that
'my Christian engagement ... obligeth me to the strict discipline of my Lord ... *to walk in newness of life*'.[84]

The fact is that this type of religious practice, detailed in its
inward application and in its outward execution is everywhere in the seventeenth century and examples could be mul-
tiplied. We find it in Taylor's *Golden Grove* (1655) which
owes its structure to the banned catechism – things to be
believed, things to be done, things to be prayed for – and
which seeks 'that religion may be conveyed, in all its
material parts'.[85] It is the whole basis of Taylor's *The Great*

Exemplar (1649) which is not only about the life of Christ but about the Christian's imitation of Christ in the daily setting of life where the chief aid in this demanding spirituality is the eucharist: 'As the sun among the stars ... so is this action, among all the instances of religion'.[86] Here in *The Worthy Communicant* this five-fold spirituality declares itself in every chapter and I believe that if we would understand and enter into the devotional context of the eucharist as the period experienced it we must appreciate how deep is the influence of a moral/ascetical theology of growth in the new life on how Anglicans prepared for, understood and participated in what happens at Holy Communion. A distinctive spirituality confronts us everywhere and, as I wrote elsewhere, 'There is a real sense in which one may say that this spirituality of the five Ds and this moral/ascetical theology are mutated presentations each of the other'.[87] Thus we begin to understand how for Jeremy Taylor the mystery demands and requires the moral and the practical: 'We must firmly purpose to amend all, to sin no more, to lead a *new life* in all solid and material practices of virtue'.[88]

This emphasis on preparation became increasingly part of the Anglican pattern more especially because, during the Commonwealth, some parishes had been almost totally deprived of the sacrament and, on the other hand, the effect of the *Directory* was virtually to impose 'closed' communions for the elect. When the need was beginning to be felt Taylor had already set about meeting it with his *Holy Living* (1650) of which Section X is devoted to 'preparation to the Holy Sacrament' the celebration of which 'is the great mysteriousness of the Christian religion'.[89] It became one of the most popular devotional works of the age, going into seventeen editions before the close of the century. Later, both Wesley and Keble acknowledged its influence on their lives.

At the heart of the eucharistic mystery is the unique high priesthood of Jesus who 'sits perpetually, re-presenting to the Father that great effective sacrifice' which in our manner and proportion we proclaim 'by sacramental re-presentation ... and offer to God and re-present in this solemn prayer and sacrament, Christ as already offered'. Thus receiving Christ we offer ourselves, our obedience and thanksgiving to the Father and so priest and people 'are sacrificers too in their manner'. What we are caught up in then, says Taylor, is a mystery begun on earth continuing in heaven and ever echoing back in human lives and this is what happens at Holy Communion for the eucharist 'is the sum of the greatest mystery of our religion; it is the copy of the passion, and the ministration of the great mystery of our redemption'.

Immediately the mystery evokes echoes and responses of practicality – repentance, purpose of amendment, self-examination, devotion: 'It is not the preparation of two or three days that can render a person capable of this banquet: for in this feast, *all Christ*, and Christ's passion and all his graces, the blessings and effects of his sufferings, are conveyed'. Sins and habits of sins must be confronted and spiritual counsel sought when needed: 'To make all this good to thee, there is nothing necessary on thy part but a holy life, and a true belief of all the sayings of Christ; amongst which, indefinitely assent to the words of institution, and believe that Christ, in the holy sacrament, gives thee his body and his blood. He that believes not this is not a Christian'.

All this 'inquisition into his life' is the indispensable preparation but Taylor thinks preparatory devotion and 'setting apart ... time ... beforehand' is also necessary: 'we are to make our souls more adorned and trimmed up with circumstances of pious actions and special devotions ... (for) ... this is thy soul's day, a day of traffic and intercourse with heaven'.

Then he turns back again from the practical to the mystery: 'These holy mysteries are offered to our senses, but not to be placed under our feet; they are sensible but not common'. At the eucharist we are beholding a mystery, 'that the Son of God should become food to the souls of his servants' and by grace we participate in the mystery that 'He should bring thee to life ... and make thee partaker of the Divine nature'.

The elements are 'not common bread and wine, but holy in their use, holy in their signification, holy in their change, and holy in their effect ... dispute not concerning the secret of the mystery, and the nicety of the manner, of Christ's presence; it is sufficient to thee that Christ shall be present to thy soul as an instrument of grace'. And at once the mystery overflows into the moral and the practical and the Monday morning of duties and relationships appears: 'Remember, that now Christ is all one with you; and, therefore, when you are to do an action consider how Christ did, or would do the like; and do you imitate his example, and transcribe his copy, and understand all his commandments, and choose all that he propounded ... for then you do every day communicate'. As one reads *Holy Living* one recalls Sir Edmund Gosse's comment in respect of *The Great Examplar* and one agrees that Taylor's was 'the most gracious voice then to be heard in England'.

Seven years later there appeared one of the greatest best-sellers of the age *The Whole Duty of Man* (1657) which became a religious force with an enormous and continuing circulation in these islands reaching its 28th edition in 1790. My own copy was printed in Dublin in 1727. Like *Holy Living* it is built around 'soberly', duty to self, 'righteously', duty to the neighbour, and 'godly', duty to God, so familiar from the General Confession in the Prayer Book. Though it is totally different in style and presentation it reveals the same detailed spirituality of discipline and devotion but cast in a minor key and that warmth and that touch of the ineffable which are part of Taylor's magic are missing. It presents a matter-of-fact piety or, in the author's words, 'a short and plain direction to the very meanest readers, to behave themselves so in this world, that they may be happy for ever in the next'.[90] The book has a certain pedestrian flavour in its presentation and there is an absence of vision and imagination, yet it converted Charles Simeon, and the deeply devotional Thomas Ken recommended it to the schoolboys of Winchester. Its view of religion is a solid and reasoned integration of faith and practice but we do well to remember that for Taylor also the goal was 'the solid and material practices of a religious life'. The difference in the two presentations is a matter of depth and of temperament and, of course, of style.

If we ask ourselves how such a book became such a force right on through the eighteenth century so that, in C. J. Stranks's phrase 'Anglicanism meant in doctrine the Bible and the Prayer Book, in practice *The Whole Duty of Man*',[91] part at any rate of the explanation lay in the fact that people had had more than enough of transports, theological disputes and near-anarchy, liturgically speaking. They were drawn to a simply and clearly written book 'which sits so firmly on the ground'. Nobody really knows who wrote it though opinion now favours Richard Allestree but whoever he was he seems to have matched the hour so that *The Whole Duty of Man* achieved vast popularity and was to be found in every respectable household and was presented to the candidate for confirmation.

The fact is, though this is rarely if ever remarked, that the book, like *Holy Living*, is a layman's book of 'practical divinity'. Divided into seventeen Sundays, it covers such subjects as faith, love, patience, humility, trust in God, prayer, repentance, fasting, pride, contentedness, chastity, temperance, justice and all the branches of duty to others. Sunday III is devoted to the eucharist, 'of preparation before, as examination: of repentance, faith, obedience: of duties to be done at the receiving, and afterwards'. The overall stance here and throughout the book is that of a covenant-theology so familiar to us in Thorndike, Taylor, Hacket and others – God's part, 'His mercies' and our part, 'our duties'. *The Whole Duty of Man* then provides a detailed and demanding preparation set in this covenant framework, rich in practical applied divinity and that combination of detailed devotion and disciplined duty both of which are essential elements in the Anglican spirituality of the century. All this is reinforced by a couple of pages on the usefulness of a spiritual guide and of confession and absolution, and 'God knows it is not only doubtful persons to whom this advice might be useful', (21) – (23). Sins and their degrees, habits, the necessary humiliation of self-examination as a prelude to contrition and repentance, all are analysed and 'you must then give a bill of divorce to all your old beloved sins' (15). The comfort of prayer, the strengthening of graces by the Holy Spirit, 'the most necessary grace ... of devotion', are then set out so as to lead into 'what is to be done at the time of receiving' (24).

It is only at this point that mystery breaks surface and in one form, the vivid depiction of 'those bitter sufferings of Christ, which are set out to us in the Sacrament: When thou seest the Bread broken, remember how his blessed Body was torn with nails upon the Cross; when thou seest the Wine poured out, remember how his precious Blood was split there; and then consider, it was thy sins that caused both ... thou hast, as much as in thee lay, crucified him daily ... a most tender and merciful Saviour'. (24) The communicant is exhorted 'to think of these sufferings again, to stir up thy faith ... to raise thy thankfulness ... to stir up this Love'. 'God reaches out to thee so precious a treasure ... on condition that thou perform thy part of the Covenant'. (25)–(28). Nothing is said to link the eucharistic action with the Heavenly Intercession and nothing is said as to whether change occurs in the elements. Only the benefits of devout and worthy reception are spoken of at length though these, of course, are a vital part of the mystery of the eucharist. It is a remarkably influential book which made a lasting impact though the theological reach, the intimate personalising of religious practice, the spiritual depth and the sensitivity to the numinous of Taylor are simply not there. This is religion in workaday clothes and none the worse for that as the use of *The Whole Duty of Man* by successive generations testifies.

Another indirect testimony is the way in which the book's title was plagiarised. For example, there were *The Whole Duty of a Christian* and *The Whole Duty of a Woman* and even Jeremy Taylor helped himself with *The Whole Duty of the Clergy* (1667). But the most interesting for our subject was *The Whole Duty of a Communicant* (1681) believed to have been written by John Gauden (1605–1662) who may well have thought to supplement what he would have seen as the deficiencies of *The Whole Duty of Man* in respect of the eucharist. The work went into numerous editions and central to its presentation of the mystery of the eucharist is the affirmation in clear terms of Christ's true, real and actual presence in the sacrament, perceived but not created by faith: 'We deny not a true and real presence and perception of Christ's body and blood in the sacrament, which in reality even they of the other gross opinion do not imagine is to sense, but to faith; which perceives its objects as really according to faith's perception as the senses do theirs after their manner. I believe, therefore, that in the sacrament of the Lord's Supper there are both objects presented to and received by a worthy receiver. First, the bread and wine in their own nature and substances distinct do remain as well as their accidents, which are the true objects of our sense ... also there are spiritual, invisible and credible, yet most true and really present, objects of faith, the body and blood of Christ, that is, Christ Jesus himself'. From the mystery flow the moral and the spiritual benefits resulting from the union with and the indwelling of Christ in the soul of the communicant 'where thou mayest unite me to thyself for ever'.[92]

Preceding *Holy Living* and *The Whole Duty of Man* in point of time was the most stupendously successful book of this type, *The Practice of Piety*, a devotional and directional manual by Lewis Bayly, Bishop of Bangor. The first edition known to be published was in 1612 and by 1734 fifty eight editions had appeared and that was not the end.[93] Translated into French, German, Hungarian, Polish and Welsh it had a marked influence on John Bunyan and as we have seen on the other side of the Irish sea it was the book which first brought James Bonnell to 'the proposal of a methodical course of religion'. More space is devoted to the Holy Communion than to any other subject, one eighth of the book dealing with the theology of the eucharist, self-examination and lengthy preparation. This is set within the pattern of piety which would become ever increasingly familiar in the devotional manuals as the century progressed – meditation and prayer as a daily regime covering all the actions of the waking hours with right doctrine governing all, repentance and works of charity, helping the poor and the sick. The public worship of our 'Holy Mother the Church' is central to the Christian life and at its centre is the sacrament where 'the whole Christ, with all his benefits, (is) offered to all, and given indeed to the faithful'.[94] Bayly says more about the elements and the eucharistic action than does *The Whole Duty of Man*. He is clear that 'The Divine Words of Blessing do not change or annihilate the substance of the Bread and Wine; (for if their Substance did not remain, it could be no Sacrament) but it changeth them in use and in name: For that which was before but common Bread and Wine, to nourish Men's Bodies; is after the Blessing destinated to an holy use, for the feeding of the Souls of Christians'. The benefits are then lifegiving and lifechanging: 'the same instance of time that the worthy Receiver eateth with his mouth the Bread and Wine of the Lord; he eateth also with the Mouth of his Faith, the very Body and Blood of Christ. Not that Christ is brought down from Heaven to the Sacraments, but that the Holy Spirit by the Sacrament lifts up his mind to Christ'.[95]

The Christian's duty in life is gone over and grace is sought in the lengthy preparation and in the eucharist is given to the faithful communicant. Unlike Taylor, Thorndike and others no change is specified in the consecrated elements through which 'the whole Christ, with all his benefits' is given and it is probably accurate to say that for Bayly the mystery of the eucharist is chiefly seen in the change it brings about in the lives of those who, through grace, seek 'to lodge so blessed a Guest in so unclean a stable'. It is what Hooker meant when with much greater depth he spoke of 'a kind of transubstantiation in us, a true change both of soul and body' which comes about through 'Christ assisting this heavenly banquet with his personal and true presence' changing the elements by 'his own divine power ... and maketh them that unto us which otherwise they could not be; that to us they are thereby made such instruments as *mystically yet truly, invisibly yet really*, work our communion or fellowship with the person of Jesus Christ'.[96]

Clearly, the Anglican writers took the preparation for what happens at Holy Communion with enormous seriousness, possibly exaggeratedly so from our point of view today. To enter fully into how indissolubly they linked 'the mysterious sacrament' with the morality of a new kind of life, we have to bear in mind that under and through and in all the detailed devotion and conscientious self-examination is the simplicity of a deepseated conviction as voiced in *The Great Exemplar*: 'Our obedience, united to the obedience of Jesus, is all our title to acceptance'. Ultimately, the Life that changes lives by indwelling is the horizon in which they set the eucharist and this was impressed on every generation at every celebration by the Book of Common Prayer: 'that we may evermore dwell in him, and he in us'.

The impact of this emphasis on preparation on the ordinary churchgoer can be guessed at from the extremely wide circulation of books like *A Week's Preparation towards a Worthy Receiving of the Lord's Supper* (1679) and *The New Week's Preparation for a Worthy Receiving of the Lord's Supper* (1749). The earlier and very popular manual centres its devotional exercises on the real spiritual presence of the Body and Blood of Christ, presented to and received by the faithful communicant: 'Christ, to show his love towards us, has given us of his own bread, and of his own cup; nay he hath given us His own body as bread, his own blood as wine for the nourishment of our souls'.[97] Circulated well on into the following century it was succeeded by *The New Week's Preparation* which was deliberately revisionist in one respect. The view of the author, who values and admits to being influenced by *The New Whole Duty of Man*, is that *The Old Week's Preparation* and books like it encouraged 'unnatural heats and ecstatic fervours, such as are a disgrace and reproach to the dignity of a rational nature' and his duty and purpose is 'to explode that fulsome and luscious method' the result of which is to make honest people 'despair of ever succeeding in the business of religion'. He quotes with approval Stillingfleet's strictures on 'this mystical divinity'.[98] This however does not affect his constantly expressed description of 'the holy eucharist' as 'this great mystery', this 'strange, high and prodigious mystery', 'that holy mystery', 'this mystery of our salvation', 'these holy mysteries', and speaking of the need for frequent communion he writes 'the mystery will affect thy wondering mind at every repetition'. As in *The Whole Duty of Man* there are meditations in dramatic phrases on the Passion.

The book provides prayers at waking, rising and dressing and self-examination with some very blunt personal questions. Like *The Whole Duty of Man*, the threefold duty is central to a structure which provides short meditations, as on the Resurrection, 'to excite a due veneration for the holy sacrament'. Confession to a priest is recommended when necessary as is daily attendance at church when possible. The imitation of Christ is the goal: 'thy grace my guide and assistance, thy goodness my pattern and example'.[99] The communicant is to pray for 'such longing desires of being made conformable to thy holy will, as may transform me into thy divine image'.[100]

The test for being 'a meet partaker of that holy mystery' is 'if I endeavour to live as becomes a Christian; if I really believe the Christian religion and sincerely govern my life by the doctrines and precepts of the Gospel'. This being so 'it is very advisable that my lamp should be trimmed',[101] hence the need for a careful and honest preparation: 'I come to thy altar to renew my baptismal covenant, of which this sacrament is a seal'.[102]

The mystery of the eucharist and this inclusive spirituality and ordered behaviour are bound together in a relationship which is as much reciprocal as causal: 'by that supernatural grace, which we receive from this spiritual food, to enable us for the better performance of our Christian duty for the future, our souls are also refreshed'.[103]

As he comes to link the real presence and the elements with the graces and the duties the author in the Second Part insists that the fault of many devotional books, including *The Old Week's Preparation* is that they 'raise and inflame the devotion of communicants, without taking any thought about *informing* and *settling* their understandings'.[104] 'You are to *understand*', he writes, that the eucharistic action is in remembrance of the Sacrifice 'esteeming and receiving these elements, not as common bread and wine, but as consecrated to represent the body and blood of Christ, to all spiritual intents and purposes; and firmly believing that you shall verily and indeed partake of all those blessings and graces, which Christ merited for mankind by his death'.[105] He finds himself in something of a quandary, I think, when he comes to discuss the words of the Catechism, 'the body and blood of Christ, which are verily and indeed taken and received'. It does not seem too much to say that, directly and indirectly, through this phrase and its companion, 'Only after a heavenly and spiritual manner; and the mean, whereby they are taken and received is Faith', the Prayer Book Catechism permeates and governs Anglican thought and writing on the eucharist. So, he leans on 'remembrance' implying 'bodily absence' and so warns: 'guard against that doctrine, which

teaches, that we eat the *natural* body'. Of course, the Catechism never thought that we do nor does it make worthy
reception dependent on remembrance but on faith.[106] The
raising of the question of the natural body as late as the mid-
eighteenth century is revealing and informative because
behind it lies an explanation of the constantly reiterated
rejection by Anglican theologians of what they variously
termed a corporal, a carnal or a local presence. The problem
had crystallized when, as Taylor noted in *The Real Presence*,
I (8), 'the word *real* is taken for *natural*'.

The long shadows cast by the Council of Rome in 1059
reached into the seventeenth century and beyond. Pope
Nicholas II had forced Berengar to accept a formulation
designed to affirm a true real presence but which was rawly
physical in its expression. Berengar was no mere symbolist,
holding as he did that consecration effects a change, but
he refused the term *sensualiter*, i.e. that it occurred in the
realm of the five senses. Moreover, and this bears closely on
our theme in this book, 'he thought the formula of 1059
eliminated the religiously vital idea of *mysterium*' as Henry
Chadwick has observed in his masterly commentary *Ego
Berengarius*. Now leaving to one side its conceptualization
the basis of which they rejected, the Anglicans knew perfectly
well that Aquinas had affirmed an essentially spiritual and
not a local presence, and they said so. But they also knew
what had been happening in theological formulation and in
popular devotional and controversial writing during the sixteenth century and afterwards. They saw that a change had
been taking place in the eucharistic controversy during the
reign of Edward VI, tragic in its eventual outworking, and
which in essence negatived the effect and content of the doctrine of transubstantiation as it had been developed in the
thirteenth century. This change, far-reaching in its impact on
any efforts at mutual understanding, was the introduction of
the phrase 'natural body' and even 'material body' into statements of belief and articles of indictment alike. Both

Bramhall and Taylor, for example, had commented on and seen the relevance of the Berengarian controversy to the perceived situation in their own times when, as C. W. Dugmore has shown, many Roman Catholic publications reflected this development. The situation appeared to confirm their suspicion that the doctrine of transubstantiation was always open to the danger of being misinterpreted as a miraculous physical change in the bread and wine. This is what underlies the constantly expressed Anglican anxiety about the phrase 'natural body'. Today, the problem has been put to rest as in the ARCIC I *Elucidation* (6): '*Becoming* does not here imply material change ... it does not imply that Christ becomes present in the same manner that he was present in his earthly life. It does not imply that this *becoming* follows the physical laws of this world'. Not so in the seventeenth century when the effects continued and were the subject of debate at the Savoy Conference of 1661 resulting in the inclusion of the sentence 'any Corporal Presence of Christ's natural Flesh and Blood' in the final rubric of the 1662 Book of Common Prayer. Already in 1604 and echoing Article XXVIII the addition of the questions and answers on the sacraments, the work of Dean Overall of St Paul's, had ensured that Anglican formularies excluded this mode of expressing what happens at Holy Communion.

Having given his testimony, our author then returns to the Catechism's wording as he differentiates between real presence and natural body in the eucharistic action: 'It will be sufficient for me to believe, that the consecrated elements are both *called and made* the body and blood of Christ, so *verily and indeed*, to all *spiritual* intents and purposes, as to convey to the faithful receiver whatever grace and blessing Christ hath annexed to the due performance of those holy rites'. His definition of the real presence shows the influence of Waterland whom he admires though the latter's relational concept of the presence is every bit as 'mysterious' as is the non-physical, sacramental change of condition posited by Andrewes,

Taylor, Thorndike, Cosin, Bramhall and others: 'The *real presence*, maintained by protestants, is not the presence of Christ's natural body, but the real presence of Christ's invisible power and grace, so *in* and *with* the elements of bread and wine, as to convey spiritual and real effects to the souls of such as duly receive them'.[107] (Author's italics). In view of his approval of Waterland one cannot refrain from comment on *The New Week's* phrase '*in* and *with* the elements of bread and wine'. The second preposition accords with Waterland's continuing stress on relation and on the 'relative holiness' of the elements as a result of their consecration. The preposition 'in' however goes further and I do not think that a reading of Daniel Waterland's major work *A Review of the Doctrine of the Eucharist as laid down in Scripture and Antiquity* (1737) or of his Charge to the clergy of Middlesex on *The Sacramental Part of the Eucharist Explained* (1739) will yield an instance of its use. For him, the elements are 'causes instrumental' and they acquire 'a relative holiness' through 'His more peculiar presence'. They are 'relatively holy as having a nearer relation to God' and 'must of course be treated with a reverence and awe suitable'. In several places in the *Review* he spells out the meaning of this from different angles. Waterland was a notable expert in patristics and he has the clarity and ability of a natural teacher for making his point in a variety of ways: 'The sum is, that the consecration of the elements makes them holy symbols, relatively holy, on account of their relation to what they represent or point to, by Divine institution: and it is God that gives them this holiness by the ministry of the word ... and which really means making them his body to us'.

Elsewhere, reflecting the familiar phrase in the Catechism, he writes... 'The body and blood of Christ are taken and received by the faithful not *substantially*, nor *corporally*, but *verily* and *indeed*, this is *effectually*. *The sacred symbols are no bare signs, no untrue figures of a thing absen*t: but the force, the grace, the virtue, and benefit of Christ's body broken, and blood shed, that is of his passion, are really and effectually present with all them that receive worthily. This is all the *real presence* that our Church teaches'. Throughout his writings the elements are to be seen in the context of relationship: 'They are now no more common bread and wine, (at least not during this their sacred application) but the communicants are to consider the relation which they bear, and the uses which they serve to'. Waterland lucidly puts the eucharistic action in total context when he declares that 'the delivery of these symbols is, in construction of Gospel law, and in Divine intention, and therefore in certain effect or consequence, a delivery of the things signified'. Many of his predecessors and successors would have been satisfied with the passage in the *Charge* of 1739 that 'the sacramental bread [is] a symbol exhibitive of the one true body of Christ, viz., the natural or personal body, given and received in the Eucharist: I say, given and received spiritually, but truly and really'.

However, when he flatly denies any possibility of change in the elements one can see why Knox was unhappy and complained about this when he spoke of theologians 'rejecting the mysterious instrumentality of the symbols' and affirmed 'the mysterious character and efficacy which the natural elements ... acquired by their consecration'.

Perhaps it is exactly here that we today would profit by recalling Gore's reminder that, for the Fathers 'sign' and 'symbol' do not stand for an absent reality and we have just seen that this is precisely what Waterland has stated and meant. Rather are symbols the evidence to the senses of a divine reality actually present. In fact, says Waterland, language about change *is* allowable 'so long as symbolical language was well remembered and understood, and men knew how to distinguish between figure and verity, between signs and things ... such a change, or transmutation ... frequently occurs in the primitive writers ... within the first six centuries ... I say, while these things were so, there could be no room for imagining any change in the elements, either as to substance or internal qualities'.

The change so visualised in the Early Church was that 'the work of the Holy Ghost upon the elements was to translate or change them from common to sacred, from *elements to sacraments*, from their natural state and condition to supernatural ends and uses, that they might become *holy signs*, certain pledges, or *exhibitive symbols* of our Lord's own natural body and blood in a mystical and spiritual way ... but no change of substance, nor of inward qualities implied'. Is he not saying here that a sacramental change *does* take place, a change not only of use but a change to being a symbol exhibiting a *present* reality though *not* a sacramental change of condition such as Taylor and others affirm? It would not be too much to say that Waterland deliberately and designedly avoids the word 'in' because of possible doctrinal error and misinterpretation although being so widely and deeply versed in the Fathers he would have known very well that, as Pusey was to put it later, the patristic use of the preposition had nothing to do with locality or materiality but simply indicates a 'presence after the manner of a sacrament'. Theologians today might bring about unitive results that would surprise them if they submitted to strict analysis not only the words 'real' and 'presence' but the phrase 'a sacramental change'. In this connection directly and in respect of Waterland's reserve concerning 'in', it is relevant to note that he cites with approval Aldrich's *Reply to Two Discourses* (1687) in which the author observes that in the Church's official formularies the term 'real presence' is not used, 'yet it must not be denied but the term may be safely used among scholars, and seems to be grounded upon Scripture itself ... which when we of the Church of England use, we mean thus: A thing may be said to be really received, which is so consigned to us, that we can really employ it to all those purposes for which it is useful in itself ... and a thing thus really received may be said to be really present, two ways, either physically or morally, to which we reduce sacramentally ... In the holy Eucharist, the Sacrament is physically, the res sacramenti morally present; the elements antecedently and locally; the very body consequentially and virtually, but both really present ... When we say that Christ is present ... in the Sacrament, we do not mean in the elements, but in the celebration'. Waterland gives this the stamp of his approval and it is startling to see raised in this little-known pamphlet the very questions which in the next section we shall see canvassed in our own century. It should be taken note of too that Waterland did not stand alone on this prepositional point. Simon Patrick, as will be indicated, stressed the mystery of the eucharist but before Waterland's time he also had asserted that the presence of Christ is *with* the bread but not *in* it.

There can be no doubt that Waterland exercised a most extensive and largely beneficial influence on Anglican eucharistic thought in his day and afterwards. One can of course understand a gradually growing reaction to a theology which at first sight *seems* to evacuate the eucharistic action of that 'mysterious uniting' which such as Alexander Knox saw as its heart. Yet in reality Waterland's relational concept of the presence with its virtualist undertones is every bit as much 'the mystery of the eucharist' as is its expression in terms of a sacramental change of condition. There is something of Cranmer and of Hooker in his thought and in fact on occasion he refers to both.

By any kind of yardstick he is a significant figure and it is therefore all the more interesting to see his professed admirer appearing to deviate here from the Waterland line. Could it be, in view of *The New Week's* frequent references to the eucharist and to the elements as 'the holy mysteries', a terminology absent (I think) in Waterland's writings, that the author felt that an emphasis of value was missing?

It has been thought worth while to dwell on so popular a work because, though belonging to a period of intellectual change, it seems determined to make the concept of mystery in the eucharist 'respectable', so to speak, in the mid-eighteenth century and at the same time to insist on the need for understanding in the business of preparation. That preparation is still a 'renewal of my baptismal covenant', a desire that through the Lord's Supper, sins will be 'rooted out', 'the graces of thy Holy Spirit' renewed and that 'my whole life may be one continued act of an humble and dutiful obedience'.[108]

I suppose that what the period's heavily underlined concern with preparation is saying is that the mystery of the eucharist is in its essence undergirded by ultimate values which are recreative of personality and character. As John Spurr remarks, 'The mystery of the sacrament was eminently practical in effect'.[109]

Was the emphasis on preparation counterproductive? At this distance in time that is likely to remain an open question. Yet one calls to mind Isaac Mann's *Familiar Exposition of the Church Catechism* which went into at least sixteen editions in Ireland where the author was Bishop of Cork from 1772–1788. He writes: 'Q. Is not a certain course of devotion as well as of examination necessary to our preparation for this sacrament? A. Where there is time for a course of solemn devotion, it ought by no means to be neglected. But yet, they who live in the fear and love of God, sincerely endeavouring to do their duty, need not be afraid to communicate upon any occasion'. This looks like a clear reaction from *The New Week's Preparation* so often printed and circulated in his country.

As well as the impact of popular manuals of this sort account has to be taken of the vigorous movement in the 1680's for more frequent communion. This met with considerable success as Spurr has shown in his richly-documented *The Restoration Church of England, 1646–1689* (1991).[110] The active participants in this revival were men like Denis Granville, Thomas Comber, William Beveridge, Isaac Basire,

Barnabas Oley, Francis Turner and Daniel Brevint. Some of them supported the cause with books and the last-named in his *The Christian Sacrament and Sacrifice* (1673) had, as we shall see, produced an influential work which reads like a theological and devotional elaboration of the observation in the *Report* of the Lambeth Conference of 1988 that both 'presence' and 'sacrifice' 'are areas of "mystery" which ultimately defy definition'.[111] Throughout, Brevint is stressing that 'this holy mystery' is designed to achieve conformity of life with Christ, the sacrifice of ourselves 'cloathed with the righteousness of thy Son'. 'This great and holy mystery ... enters me into that mystical body for which he died'.

Simon Patrick too should be reckoned as part of this movement and Kenneth Stevenson has noted 'Patrick is very much part of this change in church life'.[112] He wrote no less than four books on the eucharist and significantly for our theme the first of these is entitled *Mensa Mystica* (1660) and the last is *A Treatise on the Necessity and Frequency of Receiving the Holy Communion* (1684). His covenant-theology of the eucharist emphasises the part played by the Spirit in the eucharist and in the preparation for it. 'The holy mysteries' produce a change in the communicant because Christ is really present in the eucharist. What happens at Holy Communion is that there is a real presence and a real change – the mystery issues in the moral and devotional transforming of human lives: 'The change is in our souls and not in the Sacrament; ... his presence *is with the bread*, though not *in it*. Though it be only *in us*, yet it comes *with it* unto us if we will receive him'. This is subtle, leading into a relational understanding of the real presence, though perhaps no more subtle than Taylor's 'the great mysteriousness which is the sacramental change'. Yet at the same time Patrick rejected the opinion 'that the bread of the Supper of our Lord was but a figure or remembrance of the body of Christ received by faith, and not his true and very body' and calls to witness the ever-present Catechism's 'verily and indeed taken and received'.[113] Time

and again we find the Catechism's phrases directive, de-
lineative and controlling in Anglican eucharistic theology.

Eucharist is as imbued with the ethical as it is with the
transcendental, with the paschal mystery. It embodies and
instils ethics in the Christian pattern realised through the
grace of the Saviour's death and resurrection proclaimed
every time that the eucharist is celebrated. We are reminded
of St Luke's account (22.19–27) of the Last Supper when
Jesus, present with the apostles, identified the bread and wine
with his body and blood in the context of his approaching
self-offering but linked too with the serving practice of discipleship: 'I am among you as one who serves'. In the
eucharistic celebration, the same Christ gives himself to his
faithful people. His life, transmitted through the holy gifts,
enters theirs ('As we eat and drink these holy gifts, grant ...
that he may dwell in us and we in him') transforming them
into lives of discipleship in which grace moulds personalities
and forgiveness remoulds what has been damaged. So Taylor
could affirm that at the eucharist we may dare to say, 'I live
yet not I but Christ lives in me', knowing that the same voice
said 'the evil I do not want to do – this I keep on doing'.
Because repentance and forgiveness, grace and the new life,
are inextricable components of what happens at Holy
Communion.

This conjunction is at the heart of Anglican eucharistic
faith and practice and is liturgically expressed as in the
Exhortation which the Book of Common Prayer directs 'to
be read to the people ... at the least three times in the year'.
The benefit of the sacrament is the mystical union that 'we
are one with Christ, and Christ with us'. The communicants
are bidden to give thanks to the Holy Trinity for 'the redemption of the world by the death and passion of our Saviour
Christ, both God and man' and who by 'thus dying for us'
has by his resurrection 'exalted us to everlasting life'. We
must therefore 'examine ourselves' so that we become worthy communicants and therefore to this end, 'Repent you

truly of your sins past, have a lively faith in Christ our Saviour; amend your lives, and be in perfect charity with all men; so *shall ye be meet partakers of those holy mysteries*'.

At every eucharist the communicant hears the familiar words of the Invitation pressing home as preparatory to receiving these holy gifts this same message: 'Ye that do truly and earnestly repent you of your sins, and are in love and charity with your neighbours, and intend to lead a new life ... Draw near with faith, and take this holy Sacrament to your comfort'. This new life is the Life of Christ Risen continuing in the lives of the members of his mystical Body, for, says the Exhortation, 'when we spiritually eat the flesh of Christ, and drink his blood; then we dwell in Christ and Christ in us'. The stress here is surely on the interpersonal. Participation in 'these holy mysteries' is, so to speak, authenticated by respondent practice which in its turn is vivified by what is taking place in the eucharistic action. The people gathered round the Table of the Lord are meant to be a living witness to what, in this encounter of faith, Christ the living Lord, is doing, 'enabling Christians to avail themselves of the fruits of the once-for-all redemption'. 'Interpersonal' seems a cold, almost a clinical, term and yet it manages to catch something of that profoundly person-to-person relationship which by grace through faith is at the centre of the mystery of the eucharist and to which the Prayer Book Exhortation points – 'we are one with Christ, and Christ with us'. It is what, in his poem *The Holy Communion*, George Herbert (1593–1633) seeks to express, 'To me dost now Thyself convey':

> Onely Thy grace, which with these elements comes,
> Knoweth the ready way,
> And hath the privie key,
> Op'ning the soul's most subtile rooms;
> While those, to spirits refin'd, at doore attend
> Dispatches from their friend.

As we cast our minds back over this range of affirmations and interpretations, it is borne in upon us that for Anglican eucharistic theology and spirituality, mystery and morality are concomitants. There is a spiritual reciprocality and even a causality. There comes to mind what Aidan Kavanagh has so sensitively termed the 'graced commerce' between men and 'the One at whose table we sit by grace and pardon'. And did not Jeremy Taylor say the same? 'When the day of the feast is come ... this is thy soul's day, a day of *traffic and intercourse* with Heaven'.[114]

The passage from Kavanagh's *On Liturgical Theology* will serve admirably as summation and *envoi*:[115]

> As Christians have traditionally understood it, their liturgy does not merely approach or reflect upon all this from without, nor does it merely circle this mystery from a distant orbit. Rather, Christians have traditionally understood their liturgical efforts to be somehow enacting the mystery itself, locking together its divine and human agents in a graced commerce, the effective symbol of which is that communion between God and our race rooted in the union of divine and human natures in Christ Jesus. In the incarnation, God welds himself to us, and us to himself, without confusion. In Christ Jesus, God becomes like us in all things except our sin. In the liturgy, God welds himself into our media of discourse without becoming subordinate either to those media or to us who must use them. Christian tradition knows that God is not restricted to a sacramental order or to rite, but he has nevertheless willed to work through these media regularly as nowhere else in creation because it is precisely in these that we work upon ourselves and construct our world. It was into these media that we introduced the snake by our sin. It is in the thick of these media that God in Christ seeks the snake out.

VII

The Plurality of the Mystery
– Convaluation

Are the insistence on 'the mystery of the eucharist' and the constant references to it and to the elements as 'the holy mysteries' then ultimately in the nature of a conversation-stopper? The writers we have been examining in whose work mystery is necessarily complementary to the whole concept of sacramentality obviously did not think so. Nor were they willing to allow reason to be excluded. In order to avoid a guilt complex about appearing contradictory when discussing the mode of Christ's presence which we affirm to be a mystery, it is quite important to make the distinction which our forbears made here. *They in no way felt themselves precluded from discussing 'the manner of the mysterious presence' but with one accord they refused to treat any definition of it as ecclesially binding* since none such was laid down in Scripture which nevertheless as a criterion rendered some views either inadmissible or defective. *So, what of us today?* Is what they were saying valid for us who share in this the most 'characteristic activity of the people of God'[116] and, as we share, affirm 'the real and unique presence of Christ ... without seeking to explain it'.[117] Are there other concepts which will help us, concepts which can open our minds to the realisation that matter is complex and that *real* experience is not limited to the definable and the measurable? Perhaps we need to go to school with Thomas Traherne (c1637–1674) in whose 'powerful perception of the way in which everything in creation, every atom of space and time can be open to the divine indwelling'.[118] Is it the case that our theology has

75

become over-intellectualized and that we need to bring into play a notion of reason which leaves room for all our faculties and intuitions acting together in harmony? Do we hear a whisper that the mystery of the eucharist is for *the whole man as embodied spirit* since what happens at Holy Communion has direct bearing on the sort of person we are becoming – 'every time we receive the blessed sacrament' says Jeremy Taylor 'we mend our pace'.[119]

It could fairly be maintained, I believe, that certain modes of thought are more congenial to our minds in this connection during this last decade of the twentieth century. Two such concepts might well be those of *'value'* and *'relationship'*. Neither of them is completely novel as far as seventeenth-century Anglican theology is concerned but the *development* of both might be 'another voice that next year's words await'.

'Inevitably such new lines of thought and systems of definition lead to fresh statements of sacramental doctrine'. So ran the report *Doctrine in the Church of England* (1938) when it introduced and discussed both the concepts referred to above. The mystery of the eucharist for all schools of thought is first set out: 'The words "Body and Blood of the Lord" are themselves recognised to be symbols which denote essentially, not a corporeal and extended object, but rather the abiding life of the sacred humanity once offered in humiliation on the Cross and glorified for ever in the Ascension'.[120] The *Report* taking account of the prevailing realist terminology of the early Church in its attitude towards the sacramental elements, reviews transubstantiation, consubstantiation, virtualism and receptionism, concepts which came into circulation at different times after the first eight hundred years during which little or no attempt was made to define the How of Christ's presence in the eucharist. It identified as the core of the matter 'the questions whether and in what way that presence is to be specially associated with the consecrated bread and wine',[121] a matter which we have been considering in the course of this study of Anglican responses. The *Report* then examines the traditional doctrine of the Real Presence and the doctrines of Receptionism and of Virtualism which comes, as it were, between these two. Behind all three, of course, stands the phrase 'the real presence' which in itself can be notoriously ambiguous. It is in the discussion of this as it relates to those three presentations of the mystery of the eucharist that the phrase already quoted about 'new lines of thought and systems of definition' occurs. The *Report* continues: 'And in particular some Anglican theologians today are putting forward tentative restatements of the doctrine of the Real Presence which have the effect of destroying the boundary-line between the older doctrine of the "Real Presence" and that of Virtualism. If, for instance, substance is identified with value, it is obvious that the doctrines of Real Presence and Virtualism become indistinguishable from one another; and the substance of the consecrated elements may be said to be for Christian faith the substance of Christ's Body and Blood, without any suggestion that they lose their physical substance or value as bread and wine. This type of doctrine may be illustrated by pointing out that a pound-note is not just an elaborately printed piece of paper, but has the value in currency of a pound sterling which fact justifies us in commonly speaking of it as "a pound". Or, again, if a thing consists in the opportunities of experience which it affords, we may argue that the bread and wine are changed by consecration, in as much as they now afford as means of communion new opportunities of spiritual experience in addition to those which they originally afford as physical objects. They may truly be said to be spiritually the Body and Blood of Christ, in so far as they afford opportunities of a spiritual partaking of His sacrificed life'.[122]

Our minds to back to Taylor's doctrine of the real, spiritual presence with its insistence on a real non-corporeal change in the elements through consecration, a sacramental change –

'the conversion is figurative, mysterious and sacramental'. His phrase has resonances for this passage of the *Report* and *Taylor's dualism in respect of the elements has more than a suggestion of convaluation*: 'It is bread, and it is Christ's body. It is bread in substance, Christ in the sacrament; and Christ is really given to all that are truly disposed, as the symbols are; each as they can; Christ as Christ can be given; the bread and wine as they can". So far as I know, Taylor does not use the term 'value', but his stress on the life-transmitting mystery of the eucharist and on 'the vital power, virtue and efficacy' of the body of Christ 'joined with the elements' suggests that he is in fact setting out an expression of the doctrine of the real presence based on the elements changed through consecration so as to be two 'realities'[123] simultaneously, 'It is bread, and it is Christ's body'. The *feeling* of convaluation is there just as Taylor's theology absorbs some of the thrust of virtualism without modifying for a moment his insistence on 'the mysterious change'. His gathering into one of 'the several understandings of this mystery' may be a valuable and valid pointer today.

Archbishop William Temple who was Chairman of the Commission on Christian Doctrine set up in 1922 would two years later publish his *Christus Veritas* (1924) in the course of which he advanced the use of the term 'convaluation' in his discussion of the mystery of the eucharist. The influence of the book on the *Report* is clear. In it, he develops the concept of effectual symbol using instead the adjective 'expressive' to mean that the spiritual reality signified is actually conveyed by the symbol. Temple goes on 'It is an instrument of the Lord's purpose to give Himself to us, as well as the symbol of what He gives. What we receive *is not limited by our capacity to understand the gift*. When with the right intention I receive the Bread and Wine, I actually receive Christ, whether I have any awareness of this at the moment or not, and always more fully than I am aware'.[124] As to the elements, they 'come by the act of consecration to be the vehicle to us of His Human Nature and Life. This is now their *value*, and therefore their true substance'.[125]

Clearly, he understands the real presence in personalist and not in entitative terms as he defines presence in terms of accessibility: 'The receiver finds, and does not make, this Presence. By means of the elements Christ is present, that is, accessible but the accessibility is spiritual, not material or local, and Christ is only actually present to the soul of those who make right use of the means of access afforded'.[126] In a note to Chapter XIII he suggests that the time has come for a provisional redefining of some of the terms used in eucharistic theology, notably, the word 'present': 'Though primarily a spatial or temporal term, it always turns out to mean accessible or apprehensible. The doctrine of the Real Presence is the assertion that by means of the consecrated elements Christ is really and fully accessible to us and apprehensible by us'. Another Anglican lay-theologian, Will Spens, in his *Belief and Practice* (1915) had also developed this new insight that the Real Presence is an 'accessibility dependent upon material objects'. Temple dismisses transubstantiation and consubstantiation as attempts to 'overcome the difficulties' and concludes 'If, however, "substance" is understood to mean Value the objections to Consubstantiation also disappear. "Convaluation" is, in fact, just what is wanted. The Bread still has the value of Bread; it has also the value of the Body of Christ'.[127] This is Jeremy Taylor's conclusion and as Temple goes on to discuss the term 'body', it is noteworthy that he refers to the passage in *The Real Presence* in which Taylor says it is the same Body but differently apprehended.

Because verities do not change, the terms of their apprehension and expression have but a limited range of variability. So, in *Essays Catholic and Critical* (1926) it is not surprising to find Will Spens in his essay on the eucharist writing of 'a special presence' which has as its primary reference the experience of grace and describing the eucharistic gifts in a way and in terms wholly comparable with those of almost all the seventeenth-century Anglicans whose responses and affirmations we are passing in review. Spens wrote: 'If what has been said in the preceding sections of this essay holds good, we are bound to say that the bread and wine are changed by consecration. They acquire a new property, namely, that their devout reception secures and normally conditions participation in the blessings of Christ's sacrifice, and therefore in His life. Regard being had to their sacrificial context, this is the natural meaning of the description of the consecrated elements, in relation to their consumption, as our Lord's body and blood – His body given for us and His blood shed for us. Outwardly, we have bread and wine; the inward part and meaning of the sacrament is that these become in this sense the body and blood of our Lord, and as such are received by His people. The act of reception requires appropriation by faith, if reception is to have its proper consequence and complete meaning; but the opportunity for reception and appropriation is afforded by the sacramental Gifts. The body and blood of our Lord are given after a spiritual and heavenly manner, not by any process separate from, and merely concomitant with, visible administration, but because the bread and wine become in the above sense (without any connotation of materialism) His body and His blood. It is true that this occurs simply in and through their becoming effectual symbols, but wherever the significance of an effectual symbol is certain and considerable we naturally think of it in terms of that significance, as well in terms of its natural properties. We do not carefully separate in thought the natural properties of a florin and its purchasing value. We tend to think of the latter as to all intents and purpose a property of the object; yet it depends simply and solely on the fact that the object is an effectual symbol. The case for a similar view of the Eucharistic symbols is, of course, infinitely stronger'. Again not surprisingly Spens asserts that 'the word "convaluation" meets the case' (3rd. ed., pp.441–3).

One cannot miss the obvious fact that this passage abounds in what we may call resonances as far as the earlier Anglican writers are concerned. We are forcefully made aware of a continuity of thought and of its expression in respect of the mystery of the Eucharist. As variously phrased, material elements have acquired by consecration a changed condition, a fresh functional capacity, bearing 'on their face the glorious character of their divine appointment'. In the phrase so frequent in our authors they have become 'the sacramental body and blood'. As he discusses this widely accepted phrase (cp. *The Final Report* of ARCIC I) and its implied concept of a non-material identity, the similarity of the thinking of Spens with that of Taylor on 'Is it the same Body?' is worthy of note: 'In the only sense in which we can still think of our Lord's glorified body as identical with His natural body, we must, however, think of His sacramental body as identical with that body. The identity between our Lord's glorified body and his natural body must be held to consist in the facts that opportunities of experience which each includes and normally conditions, are directly determined by that nature which our Lord assumed at His Incarnation; and that in each case the whole complex of opportunities of experience exists as such in immediate dependence on that nature and affords immediately an expression of it. All this is, however, also the case in regard to the Eucharistic body and blood'. We recall again Taylor's careful wording concerning 'the mysterious and sacramental conversion' and his crisp affirmation that the natural, the glorified and the sacramental body of Christ is one but differently apprehended: 'I know none else that he had, or hath ... for there is no other body, no other blood of Christ, but though it is the same which we eat and drink, *yet it is in another manner*'.

What then are we saying when we affirm that Christ is sacramentally present in the holy eucharist? We are speaking of what Spens, and Knox before him, call 'a special presence'.

We are saying that He is present in a distinctive way, neither spatially nor statically but accessibly to faith so that when 'the sacramental body and blood of the Saviour are present as an offering [and] this offering is met by faith, a lifegiving encounter results'. (*Final Report*, ARCIC I, p.15). Through the Holy Spirit's action, by the instrumentality of the effectual symbols, the eucharist embodies uniquely the living activity of the risen and glorified Christ imparting to his faithful people 'who have duly received these holy mysteries' (BCP) all the benefits of his paschal sacrifice. In the mystery of the eucharist the two complementary movements transmit the Life for the recreation of lives.

By a happy coincidence Spens in the essay referred to provides one of those references which remind us of the patristic sources of Anglican eucharistic theology. Concerning the sacramental elements he quotes Theodoret, a Father whose views Jeremy Taylor approves in some detail in *The Real Presence and Spiritual*. The words chime with so much of what we have been uncovering: 'They remain in their former substance and shape and form, and are still visible and as they were before; but they are apprehended as what they have become, and are believed and adored as being what they are believed to be'.

It is striking to find an anticipation of the use of the term 'value' in seventeenth-century eucharistic thinking in a book by Daniel Brevint (1616–1695), *The Christian Sacrament and Sacrifice* (1673) which so impressed John and Charles Wesley that they used an abridged form of it as a preface to their collection of *Hymns on the Lord's Supper* (1745), the division of hymns corresponding to the section headings of Brevint's work.[128] For Brevint the eucharist is 'one of the greatest mysteries of godliness ... a great mystery, consisting of Sacrament and Sacrifice'.[129] The elements 'are far more than an ordinary figure' and the sacrament 'makes the thing which it represents, as really present for our use, as if it were newly done'. The Bread and Wine 'besides their ordinary use, bear as it were on their face the glorious character of their divine appointment' – 'How deep and holy is this mystery'.[130] His treatment is both devotional and doctrinal and we meet the theme so constant in Taylor, 'Create in me a new heart ... O blessed Jesus, my life comes out of thy death'.[131]

The communicant is made 'partaker of Christ in another manner, than when we only hear his word'. In the eucharist we 'seek not a bare representation or remembrance. I want and seek my Saviour himself, and I haste to this Sacrament ... with a full persuasion, that these words, this is my body, promise me more than a figure: that this holy banquet is not a bare memorial only ... Indeed in what manner this is done I know not'.[132]

We meet the now familiar combination of mystery and sacramentality: 'Christ's body and blood have everywhere, but especially in this sacrament, a true and real presence ... This great and holy mystery, communicates to us the death of our blessed Lord, both as offering himself to God, and as giving himself for man, as he offered himself to God, it enters me into that mystical body for which he died ... as he offers himself to man, the holy sacrament is, after the sacrifice for sin ... the table purposely set, to receive those mercies that are sent down from his altar'.[133] Here we see the eucharist as sacrifice in terms of the Heavenly altar, the theme which is central to Taylor's theology of the mystery of the eucharist – mystery, sacrifice and presence, 'the holy table is a copy of the celestial altar'. It is central too for Brevint and in similar terms: 'So let us ever turn our eyes and our hearts toward Jesus our eternal high priest, who is gone up into the true sanctuary, and doth there continually present both his own body and blood before God, and all the true Israel of God in a memorial. In the meantime we, beneath in the church, present to God his body and blood in a memorial, that under this shadow of his cross, and figure of his sacrifice, we may present ourselves in very deed before him'.[134] As with Taylor, the whole eucharistic action re-presenting the one sacrifice is 'mystery': the manner of the presence is 'mystery': the elements are 'these mysteries'. We recognize the concepts of virtualism and of value combining with 'a true and real presence' as Brevint enlarges on what happens in Holy Communion. There is in the action of the eucharist a threefold content: 'And these three make up the proper sense of those words, *Take eat; this is my body*. For the consecrated bread doth not only represent his body, and bring the virtue of it into our souls on earth, but as to our happiness in heaven bought with that price, it is the most solemn instrument to assure our title to it'. Then he develops the idea of the conveying of a title or an estate, as did Ussher who used the word 'worth' instead of 'value' 'for the better conceiving of this mystery'.[135] Brevint continues, Christ 'delivers into our hands by way of instrument and conveyance, the blessed sacrament of his body and blood; in the same manner as kings use to confer dignities ... and as fathers bestow estates ... so the body and blood of Jesus is *in full value*, and heaven with all its glory *in sure title* made over to true Christians, by that bread and wine which they receive in the holy communion'.[136]

The italics are in the text and there is a clear substitution of the concept of value for the concept of substance and all the time it is 'the mystery of the eucharist' and the 'holy mysteries', for immediately Brevint's text resolves into a prayer: 'O Lord Jesu, who hast ordained these mysteries for a communion of thy body, a means of thy grace, and a pledge of thy glory ...'.[137]

VIII

The Plurality of the Mystery – Relationship

The second restatement referred to by the report, *Doctrine in the Church of England* is embodied in the term 'relation': 'They would not affirm that the bread and wine are in themselves at all changed by consecration, either by receiving a new substance or by acquiring any new properties which can be rightly said to be theirs. Yet they believe that in the Eucharist the bread and wine are themselves taken up into *a new spiritual relation* to the living Christ. Consecration sets them apart to be the very organ of Christ's gracious self-revelation and action towards his faithful people; and they actually become that organ in so far as, in and through these material objects and what is done with them, the life of Christ, once offered through the breaking of His body and the shedding of His blood, is now really given to be the spiritual food of Christians. The bread and wine then become the Body and Blood simply through Christ's use of them to be the very means of His self-communication. To this use they are dedicated by consecration, and in it they have that real and spiritual relation to Christ Himself which belongs to the proper meaning of the terms Christ's Body and Christ's Blood'.[138]

In *some* respects this approach is not so far from that of the *Summa Theologica* in which Aquinas lays it down that 'when we say that He is under this sacrament, we express *a kind of relationship to this sacrament*' and he speaks of '*the relationship of Christ's body to those species*'.[139] St Thomas is, of course, working with the idea of substance and he affirms that Christ's presence is through the conversion of the elements, from 'substance to substance'. The conversion is not a physical change and Christ's body is in the sacrament 'by way of substance and not by way of quantity' so that 'Christ is not in this sacrament as in a place'. He is here 'sacramentally ... after a fashion proper to this sacrament'. The conversion 'is not like natural changes, but is entirely supernatural'. In other words, what is happening at Holy Communion is the transformation of a substance and not the localisation of a presence. Aquinas is endeavouring to show (within the parameters of a thought-form not widely acceptable today) that 'the entire Christ is in this sacrament' in two ways – through this conversion and 'from natural concomitance',[140] meaning that the Body and Blood of Christ are both present in each of the consecrated elements.

These questions of presence, of mysterious change and of 'the whole Christ' being received in the sacrament are precisely those analysed by Taylor's colleague and fellow-victim of persecution, William Nicholson (1591–1672) who nevertheless dismisses 'the chimera of Thomas's brain concomitancy', in which he was echoing Laud's 'a fiction of Thomas of Aquin'. Taylor called it 'their new whimsey of concomitancy.'[141] Nicholson first published his *Exposition of the Catechism* in 1655, the year after Taylor's *Real Presence and Spiritual* appeared in print.

In his description of how 'by these symbols we receive all Christ', Nicholson avers that this is through 'the will and power of Christ, who ordained these to be means and instruments for that end' and in a succint sentence he affirms a causal relationship: 'They remain in substance what they were; but *in relation to Him* are more'.[142] There is no question but that this presence of 'the whole Christ' is a real presence: 'such a real presence must be admitted, or else the communicant *receives nothing*'.[143] The elements of mystery and sacramentality are at the core of the eucharistic action: 'For what is here represented, is verily and indeed taken and received. It is on all hands confessed that in this Sacrament there is a true and real participation of Christ, who thereby imparts Himself, even His whole entire Person, as a mystical head ... this though *mystically*, yet it is *truly*; though *invisibly*, yet it is *really* done'.[144] Once again, as so often in the course of our investigation, the influence of the Catechism declares itself.

As to the elements, Nicholson says that 'the change of these ... is wholly sacramental' and Christ is 'present in the Eucharist ... sacramentally or *relatively* in the elements'. They are not changed in substance but remain 'as before in nature'.[145] Like his friend Taylor he sets out the various explications of what happens at Holy Communion and he too desires 'to bring my pitcher and try if cool water' can reconcile the differences of those most of whose views 'in the *explication of this mystery* may receive a candid interpretation'.[146] 'Cool' is indeed a fitting word for his clinical analysis of the terms 'presence' and 'real' by means of which he defines the real spiritual presence. There are four ways, he says, in which 'Christ is said to be present': divinely, as God, and so present everywhere; spiritually, and so present in the hearts of true believers; sacramentally, and so He is present in the sacrament; corporally, and so present in Judea in the days of His flesh. Similarly, there are three ways of taking the word 'really': it is the opposite of feigned or imagined 'and imports as much as truly'; it is the opposite of the merely figurative or the barely representative 'and imports as much as effectually'; it is the opposite of that which is spiritual 'and imports as much as corporally or bodily'. He is prepared to describe the eucharistic action on this basis: 'We then believe Christ to be present in the Eucharist divinely after a special manner, spiritually in the heart of the communicants, sacramentally or *relatively* in the elements. And this presence of His is real, in the two former acceptions of real; but not in the last, for He is truly and effectually there present though not corporally, bodily, casually, locally'.[147]

No doubt, there are nuances or resonances of this in Overall's 'the Body and Blood of Christ, and therefore the whole Christ ... really present ... and really united to the sacramental signs which not only signify but also convey' and in Jeremy Taylor's 'This is not a natural, real being in a place, but a *relation to a person*'.[148] We meet it plainly put by Waterland as we have seen in the opening decades of the next century when he writes of the 'relative holiness by their consecration' of the elements which 'are now no more common bread (at least during this their sacred application) but the communicants are to consider the relation which they bear'.[149] Nor can we forget Ussher's use of the word 'relative' in the passage quoted earlier. But it is Nicholson who most clearly among the Anglican writers of the seventeenth century underlines the concept of relationship which makes an appeal today to many of those who interpret what happens at Holy Communion in personalist and not in entitative terms.

IX

A Singularity of Fact

So, *what happens at Holy Communion?* What can we today learn from the ideas and insights of the past when our forbears strove to express the inter-relationship of spirit and matter in the mystery of the eucharist as this impacts upon the concepts of 'presence' and of 'reality'? Are their conceptualizations, or some of them, still valid in the realms of devotion and doctrine, of spirituality and theology? Or are they using thought-forms which are the furniture of an outmoded system? The question is whether there emerge from this investigation some conclusions which a Christian today going to Holy Communion may find to be supportive devotionally and doctrinally in a world in which glory and mystery are at a discount and the understanding of reality is limited and impoverished. This essay has attempted an exploration of aspects of answers and of insights from within the Anglican tradition past and present. One result has been, in my view, to confirm the rightness and validity of the traditional Anglican stance which insists on the reality of Christ's presence in the eucharist but refuses to make any definition of the manner of it doctrinally mandatory. More than that, I would hold that the investigation, by revealing the riches of a variety of understandings of the eucharist, *requires* of us what Taylor (and Nicholson) regarded as 'gathering together into a union all those several portions of truth and differing apprehensions of mysteriousness'. It has surely shown that Anglicans should stop apologizing for a pluralism of legitimate interpretations. Not just legitimate but surely necessary because the eucharist as sacrament is a concretion of all that Christ is, in and for the Christian, in the riches of

His life offered for us and now offered to us through the gifts which earth has given and human hands have made.

Perhaps something else of importance surfaces as a result of this exploration of answers, namely, that the most illuminating form of our original question might well be '*What is it that Christians receive in Holy Communion?*' No sooner is it posed than, looking back over the range of responses from Overall to Temple, we perceive that the phrasing fits neither doctrine nor devotion in the Christian experience. It should be 'Who' and not 'What' and at once any valid response is seen to be in personalist and not in entitative terms. In the words of Forbes, it is 'the presence of Christ the Lord in the sacrament, Who is present in a wonderful but real manner' and who is actually received spiritually in 'these mysteries'.

The same truth is brought home to us if we frame our question from another angle: *What is the purpose of the eucharist?* The *Agreed Statement* (6) of ARCIC I replies that 'Its purpose is to transmit the life of the crucified and risen Christ to his body, the Church, so that its members may be more fully united to Christ and with one another'. Aquinas had said the same thing earlier: 'What is contained in this sacrament, which is Christ; who ... also by coming sacramentally into man, causes the life of grace, according to John 6.58: 'He that eateth me, the same shall live by me'.[150] The same text recurs in the Anglican writings and in them the thrust is the same. We are talking about a personalist view of the real presence when the living Christ gives Himself and makes us to share His being and His life through the effectual instruments which are brought into a life-transmitting relationship with Himself in the mystery of the eucharist. In other words, we are brought full circle to Hooker's and Taylor's emphasis on Christ's life entering ours through the sacrament as the modern Catechism affirms.

The body and blood means that particular life in the totality of its being, a vital personality (to use a phrase of Bishop Wand).[151] When Jesus used the words he was physi-

cally present and so was conveying to the disciples the guar-
antee that henceforth these effectual symbols would be, to
use Taylor's phrase sacramentally 'sublimed to become the
body of Christ'.[152] Moreover, Jesus linked the words not only
with His life but with the approaching sacrifice of His life and
ever since, in St Paul's phrase, the Church in the eucharist
proclaims that sacrifice. Taylor developed both aspects of
this in his *Real Presence* and his *Worthy Communicant*. He
in fact heads Section II of the latter with our second interpretation of the titular question, 'What it is, which we receive in
the Holy Sacrament'. Immediately, it becomes clear that for
him it is 'Who', Christ present, 'and so Christ is our food, so
he becomes life unto our souls'; 'our souls live a new life by
Christ, of which eating and drinking is the symbol and the
sacrament. And this is not done to make this mystery
obscure, but intelligible and easy'. This is 'the glorious mystery of our communion' and so 'Christ is their life'. Taylor
makes the point about Christ's physical presence at the Last
Supper: 'at the institution of the supper, he affirmed of the
bread and wine, that they were his body and his blood ... *in
the nature of that mystery* ... both of them were his body, but
after a diverse manner'. Christ's body 'in the holy sacrament
of the eucharist ... is present in a sense more agreeing to
sacraments'. The outward and visible sign and the inward
and spiritual grace of the sacrament are accommodated to
our nature for 'we have two lives, a natural and a spiritual;
and both must have bread for their support'. He quotes
Augustine on the elements 'it is the same and not the same;
the same invisibly, but not the same visibly' and throughout
the section the real presence of Christ is apprehensible by
faith through the elements by means of which Christ's life
enters ours: 'we must have him within us, and we must be in
him'.[153] The sacramental elements 'are made to be signs of a
secret mystery ... of Christ's body and blood ... by these his
Holy Spirit changes our hearts and translates us into a divine
nature ... (they) ... speak God's language in our accent'.

They, material objects, are part of the mystery. Perhaps we might here make a particular application of lines from the Welsh poet, R. S. Thomas:

> We are beginning to see
> now it is matter is the scaffolding of spirit.

In their 'thingness' they are essential and instrumental to what is happening in the eucharistic action because they are appointed to be part of this spiritual process and designated His body and blood in the new covenant of grace of which, says Thorndike, 'the celebration of the eucharist is the renewal'.[154]

In *The Real Presence*, Section VII, Taylor takes both points together, affirming that because Christ was present 'they ate the blessed eucharist, but it was not in remembrance of Christ's death; for it was future then'. Here *the heart of the mystery is seen to be sacramentality* for 'it follows from hence that then Christ only instituted a sacrament, or figurative, mysterious representment of a thing ... therefore it could not be a real exhibition of his body in a natural sense ... but it is wholly ritual, mysterious, and sacramental'. The eucharist then, says Taylor, is 'the sacramental image of his death' and its celebration by the Church is united with the Saviour's pleading of His sacrifice at the heavenly altar; 'as Christ in heaven represents his death in the way of intercession, so do we by our ministry'. It is from this one perfect offering that the words of institution derive their spiritual power and their sacramental effect: 'This is my body, are the sacramental words or those words *by which the mystery or the thing is sacramental* ... for they signify the death which Christ suffered in the body. *It is but an imperfect conception of the mystery* to say, it is the sacrament of Christ's body only, or his blood; but it is 'ex parte rei', a sacrament of the death of his body: and to us a participation, or an exhibition of it, as it became beneficial to us, that is, as it was crucified, as it was our sacrifice'.[155]

Sacrament and Sacrifice are indissolubly fused in the mystery of the eucharist. 'The holy sacrament' wrote Daniel Brevint 'is a great mystery, consisting of sacrament and sacrifice'.

Conclusion

Is there then a conclusion to be drawn from this survey of Anglican answers to the question 'What happens at Holy Communion?' If by this one means a formula which could summarise their content in a neat précis, the answer is in the negative. Such an attempt would be a self-defeating exercise. On the contrary, their value consists in the rich range of insights which they afford. Rather may one conclude that these responses are complementary and there is not one of them which is not capable of deepening our experience and perception of the participation in what happens at Holy Communion. There is also the conclusion that these responses in their spread of emphasis arise from a common base, the belief in the real presence of the glorified Lord who 'in the whole action of the eucharist, and in and by his sacramental presence given through bread and wine ... offers himself to his people ... In the eucharist the human person encounters in faith the person of Christ in his sacramental body and blood. This is the sense in which the community, the body of Christ, by partaking of the sacramental body of the risen Lord, grows into the unity God intends for his Church'.[156]

In the interest of unity in truth, theologians (and Churches) would do well to keep in the forefront of their minds (and of their dialogues) the considered comment in the *Report* of the 1988 Lambeth Conference that both presence and sacrifice in the eucharist 'are areas of "mystery" which ultimately defy definition'. No matter how much light is shed by theological exploration it is difficult to see how in the last resort that statement can be patient of any meaningful modification. Its practical and ecumenical relevance is as considerable as the theological impact of what it is saying about the essential nature of the eucharist. Substantial agreement is unlikely so long as its implications are put to one side and any one formulation among others is exclusively insisted upon as mandatory and definitive for Catholicity. It is after all the _mystery_ of the eucharist.

In the contemporary scene this was precisely the point made by the French Roman Catholic Episcopal Commission for Christian Unity in its general evaluation of the Holy See's _Response_ to the _Final Report_ of ARCIC I in 1992: 'We are astonished at the demands for an identity of formulations in an age when we live in a society which has become conscious of its multicultural character'. In the previous year, the present Archbishop of Canterbury had underlined 'a difference of methodology' in the _Response_. Contrasting 'consonant with faith' and 'identical with teachings', he commented 'If either Communion requires that the other conforms to its own theological formulations further progress will be hazardous'.[157] The methodology informing the work of ARCIC I arose from and grew out of the mandate given by Pope Paul VI and Archbishop Michael Ramsey of Canterbury (_The Common Declaration 1966_) for 'a serious dialogue ... founded upon the Gospels and on the ancient common traditions'. The Archbishop was later to reveal that the Pope 'put those words into the draft himself'.[158] Objectively, we are looking here at something quite fundamental, either the insistence on, even the imposition of, definitions or the agreement on the essential content of faith. Because we are talking about the mystery of the eucharist divergent 'explanations' would appear allowable and in the nature of the thing, inevitable though all are committed to the fundamental belief in that mystery. Jeremy Taylor had confronted this, concluding that what happens at Holy Communion 'is a thing impossible to be understood; and therefore it is not fit to be inquired after' and so the manner of Christ's presence in the holy mysteries 'were better ... left at liberty' since for a thousand years it had remained eccle-

Taylor

sially undefined. For him the irreducible element is mystery and the option chosen must be one which safeguards the mystery of the eucharist: 'The presence of Christ is real and spiritual: because this account does still leave the article in his deepest mystery'.[159] Has it not always been the experience of Christians that once their minds confront what happens at Holy Communion they find themselves kneeling in face of *mysterium fidei*? Was not this for Richard Hooker the last word? Only such a methodology as takes account of the areas of undefinable mystery in the whole action of the eucharist will serve – the mystery in which Jesus, the living Lord, imparts the real gift of himself. Such would appear to be a lesson to be drawn not only from this survey of Anglican responses but from the continuing story of the Christian past and present as men search for words to convey what Lancelot Andrewes calls 'the mystery of Thy dispensation'.

sacrifice?

The long history of the tradition over the centuries from the pre-Nicene Church onwards to the Middle Ages and through the Reformation period to the present time reveals the wide and sometimes contradictory range of men's efforts in expressing the mystery of the eucharist. There has been variation in, and opposition to, one aspect after another of these formulations designed in the first place to express what happens at Holy Communion: on the relation of symbols to reality, of word to matter, of language to thought. Questions have been debated concerning the nature of sacramental presence, of presence in truth and presence in mystery, of presence under a figure and concerning the content of the term 'presence' itself. There has been prolonged controversy, still continuing, as to the nature of the body of Christ in the eucharist. There was talk of impanation and talk of change of substance. There was talk of memorial symbolism. Was Christ's presence in the eucharist *spiritualiter* or *corporaliter* or *sacramentaliter*? As we have been discovering, the latter was seen as an advance by the Anglicans in that it avoided mere symbolism on the one hand and what they regarded as a carnal or corporal or local presence on the other. They insisted that a sacramental presence affirms and ensures the essential mystery of the eucharist, as does the ARCIC I *Statement*.

Apart from times of controversy and polemics when men tended to define as against one another, the goal through the centuries has been so to express the truth of the eucharistic mystery in all its fulness that the lives of God's people would be enriched as they shared in the offering of the liturgy. This has been the fundamental objective for councils, synods and individual theologians. True, there were acrid disagreements which disfigured the very nature of the Church as the body of Christ. True, some concepts were advanced which doctrinally or devotionally proved themselves to be largely unacceptable or misleading. In spite of all this, reviewing the record of Christian thought and debate on the eucharist over the years appears to give support to a feasible approach, the *quest for a convergence in essentials*, and even suggests that here a legitimate option may exist for Christians separated on the sacrament of unity.

So what are the parameters of theological legitimacy when we strive to express in truth the actual meaning of all that takes place in the holy mysteries? One calls to mind our analysis in Section IV of one method of handling and answering this question when Hooker dealt with it in terms of his core-principle of conjunction. Not so far removed from this is the passage in the ARCIC I *Elucidation* (7) the wisdom and value of which may well be more fully appreciated at some time in the future. It surely merits quotation in full: 'This transformation into the likeness of Christ requires that the eucharistic gifts be received in faith. In the mystery of the eucharist we discern *not one but two complementary movements within an indissoluble unity*: Christ giving his body and blood, and the communicants feeding upon them in their hearts by faith. Some traditions have placed a special emphasis on the association of Christ's presence with the

consecrated elements; others have emphasized Christ's presence in the heart of the believer through reception by faith. In
the past, acute difficulties have arisen when one or other of
these emphases has become almost exclusive. In the opinion
of the Commission neither emphasis is incompatible with
eucharistic faith, *provided that the complementary movement emphasized by the other position is not denied.
Eucharistic doctrine must hold together these two movements since in the eucharist, the sacrament of the New
Covenant, Christ gives himself to his people so that they may
receive him through faith*'.

Is it naive to hold that these are the legitimate parameters
and that this conjunction is a liberating answer? Have we
here the essential content?

Could it possibly be that somewhere in this simplicity

> 'Next year's words await another voice'

though always there will be that graced probing into the
ineffable

> 'Leaving one still with the intolerable wrestle
> with words and meanings'?

Yet if in the commerce of grace between God and his people
the reach of our understanding is limited, the purpose of the
eucharist, a mystery emergent from the mystery of the
Gospel, is clear to all, says the ARCIC I *Statement* (6): 'On
the one hand, the eucharistic gift springs out of the paschal
mystery of Christ's death and resurrection, in which God's
saving purpose has already been definitively realized. On the
other hand, its purpose it *to transmit the life* of the crucified
and risen Christ to his body, the Church'.

The mind goes back to Augustine: 'If you then are the body
and members of Christ, your mystery is laid on the Table of
the Lord, your mystery you receive'. His words resonate
through the generations of Anglican theologians to whom we
have been listening: 'Eat life, drink life; you will have life, and

yet the life is whole. Then this will happen, that is, the body and blood of Christ will be life to each one, if what is visibly received in the Sacrament is spiritually eaten and spiritually drunk in very truth'.[160]

> Therefore we proclaim the mystery of faith:
> Christ has died.
> Christ is risen.
> Christ will come again.[161]

NOTES TO PART ONE

1. *An Exposition of the Church Catechism* (1685).
2. *Ecclesiastical Polity*, V, lxii, 3.
3. *Preface to the Dissuasive*, *Works* (Heber ed.), Vol. X, p. cxv.
4. *A Theological Word Book of the Bible* (1950, ed. Alan Richardson), p. 156.
5. All quotations from the Introduction to *The Worthy Communicant*, *Works* (Heber ed.), Vol. XV, pp. 397–403.
6. Thomas K. Carroll, *Jeremy Taylor: Selected Works* (1990), p. 55, and Olivier Clément, *The Roots of Christian Mysticism* (1993), pp. 9–10, 35–37, 76–91, 115–129.
7. *Works*, Vol. VI, p. 121.
8. Venice working documents of ARCIC I published in *Theology* (1971).
9. *Ecclesiastical Polity*, V, lxvii, 1.
10. *The Worthy Communicant*, Section III.
11. *Works*, Vol. V, p. 421.
12. *Works*, Vol. XV, p. 412.
13. *Works* (L.A.C.T.ed.), Vol. IV, pp. 35–6, 73.
14. From *The Real Presence and Spiritual* (1654), *Works*, Vol. IX, p. 421.
15. ib.
16. *Responsio*, C.I.1.
17. *Works* (L.A.C.T.ed.), Vol. I, p. 7.
18. Discourse IX of *The Great Exemplar* (1649), *Works*, Vol. III, pp. 290–294.
19. *Works*, Vol. IX, pp. 424–5.
20. *Works*, Vol. IX, pp. 424–5.
21. Darwell Stone *A History of the Doctrine of the Holy Eucharist* (1909), Vol. 2, pp. 192–3.
22. Quoted in Essay 4 (C.W. Dugmore) in *Eucharistic Theology Then and Now* (1968), pp. 68–9.
23. *Works* (L.A.C.T.ed.), VIII, 263–5.

24. Quoted in C.W. Dugmore *Eucharistic Doctrine in England from Hooker to Waterland* (1942), pp. 46–7.
25. *Works*, Vol. X, p. 61.
26. Kenneth Stevenson, *Covenant of Grace Renewed* (1994), pp. 77–83.
27. cp. C. W. Dugmore, loc.cit., pp. 102–110.
28. See C.W. Dugmore, loc.cit., p. 80, for the references in Bramhall's *Works* (L.A.C.T.ed.), and cp. Darwell Stone, II, pp. 338–340.
29. *Works*, Vol. IX, p. 423.
30. H. R. McAdoo, *The Eucharistic Theology of Jeremy Taylor Today* (1988), p. 116.
31. *The Final Report* (1982), pp. 15, 21.
32. *The Final Report* (1982), p. 15.
33. *The Worthy Communicant*, *Works*, Vol. XV.
34. *The Worthy Communicant*, Ch. I, Sections I, II, *Works*, Vol. XV, pp. 407, 410.
35. John Bunyan, *The Pilgrims Progress* (1678/1685) The Second Part.
36. Austin Farrer, *Saving Belief* (1964), pp. 14–16.
37. All quotations from *Ductor Dubitantium*, Ch. II, Rule III, *Works*, Vol. XI, pp. 430–464.
38. See my *Eucharistic Theology of Jeremy Taylor Today* (1988), pp. 190–1.
39. *Ductor Dubitantium*, Ch. II, Rule iii, para. 63, *Works*, Vol. XI.
40. ib., para. 61.
41. *Golden Remains of the ever memorable Mr John Hales* (1659), pp. 7, 31.
42. Richard Hooker, *Ecclesiastical Polity*, V, LXVII, (1) (12).
43. Quoted in *Anglicanism* (1935), ed. More and Cross, pp. 488–9.
44. *Eucharistic Doctrine in England from Hooker to Waterland* (1942), pp. 53–4.
45. *Works* (1847/52 ed.), Vol. IV, p. 487.
46. Quotations from *Considerationes Modestae* (posthumously published in 1658 and edited by Bishop Sydserf who ordained Brevint and Durel in Paris). The translation is from Darwell Stone, *A History of the Doctrine of the Holy Eucharist* (1909), Vol. II, pp. 305–8.
47. By the Revd Peter Barrett, Chaplain of Trinity College, Dublin, who is preparing a thesis on Knox.
48. *An Inquiry into Eucharistic Symbols*, pp. 38–9, 89. For Palmer, Keble and Pusey references see Darwell Stone, loc.cit., II, pp. 521–540; See also, John Keble, *On Eucharistic Adoration*. (3rd ed. 1867), pp. 4, 7, 58, 95–121, 138–143, 176, 238–310; E. B. Pusey, *The Doctrine of the Real Presence* (1883 ed.), passim and pp. 95, 131–2, 211; R. I. Wilberforce, *Sermons on Holy Communion* (1854), pp. 125–6, 128–9, 139, 199–229, 266–7, 283–8.
49. ib. p. 13.
50. ib. pp. 90–1.
51. ib. pp. 65–66.

52. ib. p. 62.
53. ib. pp. 70–1.
54. ib. pp. 55, 59 and cp. p. 44.
55. ib. p. 45.
56. ib. p. 41.
57. ib. pp. 15–16.
58. ib. pp. 70–1, 91.
59. ib. pp. 46, 49 and cp. p. 13.
60. ib. p. 79.
61. ib. p. 90.
62. William Hamilton, *The Exemplary Life and Character of James Bonnell Esq., Late Accomptant General of Ireland* (3rd ed. 1707), pp. 247, 254. For an assessment of Bonnell's religion see H. R. McAdoo 'The Religion of a Layman: James Bonnell', *SEARCH*, Vol. 14, No. 1, Spring 1991, and H. R. McAdoo *Anglican Heritage: Theology and Spirituality* (1991), pp. 25–31.
63. *Life*, p. 242.
64. ib. p. 212.
65. ib. p. 215.
66. ib. pp. 166–7, 168–175.
67. *Works*, Vol. 2, pp. 190–1.
68. *Works*, Vol. 3, pp. 296–8.
69. *Works*, Vol. 15, p. 590.
70. *Works*, Vol. 15, p. 403.
71. *Works*, Vol. 15, p. 424.
72. ib. p. 413.
73. ib. pp. 424–5.
74. ib. p. 449.
75. ib. p. 672.
76. ib. pp. 457–8.
77. ib. p. 479.
78. ib. p. 530.
79. *Unum Necessarium*, Preface and Ch. III, 1.
80. Sermon III Ad Clerum, n. 34: Vol II, p. 105 and cp. Sermon IX Ad Aulam, n. 28, Vol. 1 p. 242 (Oxford 1884).
81. For fuller treatment and analysis see my *Anglican Heritage: Theology and Spirituality* (1991) and my *First of Its Kind: Jeremy Taylor's Life of Christ. A Study in the Functioning of a Moral Theology* (1994).
82. *Works*, Vol. 15, pp. 531–533.
83. *The Practice of True Devotion, in Relation to the End, as well as the Means of Religion.* The signed preface was added to the second edition in 1715 though the preface is dated 1708. The book, designed 'for the poorer sort, for whose use this undertaking was chiefly engaged in', went into at least seventeen editions.
84. See Chapters IV and V.
85. *Works*, Vol. 15, pp. 1–76.

86. *The Great Exemplar*, Discourse XVI (on the eucharist), *Works*, Vol. 3, pp. 173–185.
87. H. R. McAdoo *First of its Kind: Jeremy Taylor's Life of Christ* (1994), p. 125.
88. *The Worthy Communicant*, *Works*, Vol. 15, p. 532.
89. *Works*, Vol. 4, pp. 265–275.
90. Preface, Sect. I. The edition here used is a Dublin printing of 1727.
91. C.J. Stranks, *Anglican Devotion* (1961), p. 144.
92. Darwell Stone, loc.cit., Vol. II, pp. 459–460.
93. For a fuller evaluation of *The Practice of Piety* see C.J. Stranks, *Anglican Devotion* (1961), pp. 35–63.
94. *The Practice of Piety* (1711, 50th edition), p. 277.
95. ib. p. 276, 286.
96. ib., p. 303; E.P.V. LXVII, II.
97. Stone, loc.cit. Vol. II, p. 458.
98. *The New Week's Preparation*, The Author to the Reader, (Dublin printing, 1812), pp. i–iv.
99. loc.cit., p. 88.
100. ib., p. 108.
101. ib. pp. 48–9.
102. ib., p. 109.
103. ib., p. 17.
104. loc.cit., Part the Second, p. 5.
105. ib., p. 17.
106. ib., pp. 35–37. For a detailed discussion of the 'natural body' see my *The Eucharistic Theology of Jeremy Taylor Today* (1988), pp. 119–126; see also C. W. Dugmore, loc.cit., pp. 23–29, pp. 121–132; for the Berengarian controversy see Henry Chadwick, 'Ego Berengarius', *Journal of Theological Studies* 40 (1989), pp. 414–45.
107. ib., pp. 38–9.
108. ib. pp. 42–3.
109. *The Restoration Church of England* (1991), p. 295.
110. loc.cit., pp. 360–1, 364–9. This work must become a source-book for the study of the period.
111. *The Truth Shall Make You Free*, The Lambeth Conference 1988, *Report*, p. 211.
112. *Covenant of Grace Renewed* (1994), p. 154.
113. For quotations see C.W. Dugmore's assessment of Patrick in *Eucharistic Doctrine in England from Hooker to Waterland* (1942), pp. 112–116: cp. also Kenneth Stevenson, loc.cit., pp. 149––160.
114. *Holy Living*, X, 7.
115. Aidan Kavanagh, *On Liturgical Theology* (1984), p. 120.
116. Edward Knapp-Fisher, *Eucharist: Many-sided Mystery* (1988), p. 97.
117. *The Lima Report.*

118. A. M. Allchin, *The Joy of all Creation* (1993), p. 108.
119. *Works*, Vol. XV, p. 590.
120. loc.cit., pp. 174–5.
121. ib., p. 168.
122. ib., pp. 175–6.
123. cp. *The Eucharistic Theology of Jeremy Taylor Today* (1988), pp. 177–182.
124. *Christus Veritas* (1924), p. 239.
125. loc.cit., p. 260.
126. ib., pp. 240–1.
127. ib., pp. 245–249.
128. For a fuller treatment see H.R. McAdoo 'A Theology of the Eucharist: Brevint and the Wesleys', *Theology*, July/August 1994 Vol. xcvii No. 778, pp. 245–256.
129. *The Christian Sacrament and Sacrifice*, Extracted from a late Author by John Wesley (London 1784) Sect. I.
130. loc.cit., Sect. II.
131. ib., Sect. III.
132. ib., Sect. IV.
133. ib., Sect. IV.
134. ib., Sect. VI, in which the heavenly altar and the holy table theme is fully developed by Brevint.
135. Quoted in More and Cross, *Anglicanism* (1935), p. 489.
136. ib., Sect. V, (5), (6).
137. ib., Sect. V, (7).
138. loc.cit., pp. 176–7.
139. S.T. III, III, Q. 76, Art. 6.
140. Quotations from S.T. III, III, Q. 75 and Q. 76.
141. W. Nicholson, *An Exposition of the Catechism of the Church of England* (1685), Parker ed. 1842, p. 180: W. Laud, *Works* (L.A.C.T.ed.), II, p. 338: Taylor, *Works*, Vol. 9, p. 438.
142. *Exposition*, pp. 185, 188.
143. loc.cit., p. 179.
144. ib., p. 183.
145. ib., p. 177.
146. ib., p. 178.
147. ib., p. 179.
148. *The Real Presence*, Sect. XI (13) where Taylor is discussing Aquinas with approval on 'Christ's body is sacramentally in more places than one, which is very true'.
149. C.W. Dugmore, loc.cit., p. 175.
150. S.T., III, III, Q. 79, A. 1.
151. Bishop William Wand, 'Anglican Eucharistic Theology in the Twentieth Century', *The Alcuin Club Report*, 1972–3, p. 11.
152. *The Real Presence*, *Works*, Vol. 9, p. 476.
153. All quotations from *The Worthy Communicant*, Section II, *Works*, Vol. 15, pp. 409–21.

154. *The Worthy Communicant*, Section III, *Works*, Vol. 15, pp. 430–1. Thorndike, *Works*, Vol. IV, part I.
155. *Works*, Vol. 9, pp. 493–4.
156. *The Final Report* (1982) of ARCIC I, pp. 13, 21, 22.
157. For references see *Anglicans and Roman Catholics: The Search for Unity* (1994 ed. Christopher Hill and Edward Yarnold SJ), pp. 170, 173 and compare Christopher Hill's commentary 'The Fundamental Question of Ecumenical Method' in the same volume, pp. 222–236.
158. Michael Ramsey, *The Anglican Spirit* (1991), ed. Dale Coleman, p. 138.
159. *The Real Presence and Spiritual* (1654), *Works*, Vol. IX, p. 423.
160. From St Augustine's *Sermons*, quoted in Darwell Stone, loc.cit., pp. 92, 95.
161. Eucharistic Prayer A in the American Prayer Book of 1979.

PART TWO

THE MYSTERY OF SACRIFICE

Kenneth Stevenson

I

Origins and development

If you look up the word 'sacrifice' in the Oxford English Dictionary, you are greeted with a variety of definitions of which two stand out in particular prominence. First comes the physical definition, the slaughter of an animal as an offering to God or a deity. The second is what might be called the spiritual definition, namely the offering of prayer, thanksgiving, penitence, and submission. The first may be termed the basic one, fundamental to many religions. The second may be regarded as derivative, since it looks at the motives and feelings of the worshippers in their offering of worship, whether or not they are making a physical sacrifice of an animal, or some other offering of a physical kind, such as a cereal offering.

As the New Testament shows abundantly, the image of sacrifice is in the first instance used as a way of illustrating the meaning of Christ's death. As with so much of the New Testament, the way in which this happens varies a great deal from one author to another. Mark uses the image of the 'ransom for many' (Mk 10.45b), whereas the Letter to the Hebrews indulges in a much more elaborate development of the sacrificial imagery, likening Christ to a high priest, in the eternal temple in heaven (Heb 4.14–16). At the heart of the image is the fundamental truth about sacrifice, that it is about cost, self-giving, and the benefits that accrue to those who are prepared to look upon this interpretation of life. That is why, for instance, towards the end of the Letter to the Romans, Paul exhorts his audience to offer themselves as 'a living sacrifice' (Romans 12.1) as the only response towards which faith directs us.

In that notion of 'living sacrifice', we can see how already the writers of the New Testament are grappling with the relation between the two basic definitions given earlier. Christ's death is the physical sacrifice, ours is the spiritual – not in the sense of being unreal, but rather because the relationship between Christ and his followers is derivative. All our actions, good, bad, indifferent (including worship itself) have to be seen in relation to that one, unique act of self-offering, which stands at the heart of history, and which is so central to its meaning that it is eternal in its character and implications. A 'living sacrifice', therefore, is not a contradiction in terms, for we are not dead, but alive. And we dare to pray that we may not be conformed to this world, rather transformed, by the renewing of our minds, so that we may know the will of God, what is his good and perfect will (Rom 12.2).

Seen from that wider context, it is not hard to make the more specific connection between the eternal sacrifice of Christ and the sacraments of baptism and eucharist. In baptism the new Christian spiritually dies and rises with Christ (Rom 6.3–11), and in the eucharist the Church makes the memorial of Christ's death until he comes (I Cor 11.23–26). Indeed, towards the end of the New Testament, the temple-sacrifice imagery is applied to the whole Christian life:

'Come to him, to that living stone, rejected by men but in God's sight chosen and precious; and like living stones be yourselves built into a spiritual house, to be a holy priesthood, to offer spiritual sacrifices acceptable to God through Jesus Christ.' (I Pet 2.4f.)

It was inevitable, therefore, that sacrificial imagery would come to be applied to the eucharist, not least because of the widespread practice of physical sacrifices in the religions of the ancient world. Sometimes the whole eucharist would be described as a sacrifice, as in one of the earliest manuals of Christian prayer, the *Didache*, which was probably written around A.D. 90 in Syria.[1] On other occasions, the offering of the bread and wine is actually referred to in the eucharistic prayer, as in a prayer probably written in Rome near the start of the third century in a document called *The Apostolic Tradition* of Hippolytus.[2] The link between making the memorial of Christ's death and presenting the gifts seemed to be so close as almost to require these two notions to be expressed in the same breath.

The tale of sacrificial language in relation to the eucharist is a complex one in its details, and there is no need here to retrace many steps back into the Middle Ages.[3] But it is no exaggeration to say that one of the most significant aspects of the Reformation was to deal with this aspect of the eucharist in a constructively critical manner. The main contributing factors – the result of an unfortunate set of coincidences – may be listed as follows:

1. Whereas the Churches of the East, including the Orthodox, used eucharistic prayers that held the central motifs (narrative, Kingdom, Spirit, and sacrifice) in some kind of balance, the Roman Catholic Church had only one eucharistic prayer, in which the sacrifice-offering theme was central.

2. The eucharist had for a number of centuries migrated from its earlier, popular, corporate context, to being in many cases a private service, offered by the priest, on behalf of various concerns, including the departed.

3. In many parts of Catholic Europe, there grew whole clusters of private prayers, recited by the priest at the offertory, all of which had a heavily sacrificial style.

4. So strong was the sacrificial focus that some theologians began to speak of the eucharist as an offering of Christ himself to the Father – no longer a self-offering, but an offering by the Church.

With regard to this last point, a few words of explanation may be helpful. Gabriel Biel (c.1420–1495), the first Professor of Theology at the University of Tubingen, enunciated such a view in an eloquent style when writing about the celebration of the mass. After the words of consecration, the priest offers the bread and wine, as Christ's body and blood, to the Father. It is clear that this kind of interpretation was to sow the seeds of future problems. A much milder line was taken by Thomas Aquinas (c.1225–1274), who taught that the mass was an offering, but that this was primarily focused at the presentation of the gifts at the offertory. As a Dominican, Aquinas was accustomed to a relatively simple series of prayers at this point in the service. He does place the eucharist in a direct relation to the cross, and uses vivid language, but unlike 'transubstantiation', Aquinas' view of the eucharist as a sacrifice was not so problematic to the Reformers.[4]

The Reformers took exception to the pastoral consequences of these four features, and one by one, they were overturned. The Roman eucharistic prayer had to be rewritten, or replaced by material in which the sacrificial language was considerably reduced. The eucharist should only be celebrated when there were *communicants*, thus making the celebration's primary focus the meal, rather than praying for specific needs. The offertory prayers were abolished, the bread and wine being placed on the table in a functional manner. And all the language of prayers and sermons, stressed the memorial-aspect of the eucharist, because the Church cannot 're-offer' Christ, since that happened only once (Rom 6.10, I Pet 3.18).

From a theological point of view, the two aspects of late mediaeval Catholic piety to which the Reformers were most sensitive were masses for the dead, where the eucharist was regarded as doing them some good in purgatory, and the notion of offering Christ afresh. Roman Catholic theologians have rewritten some of their own history, in order to show, for example, that the first masses for the dead were not intended to 'do something' for them, but rather to celebrate the eucharist in union with them, praying for the whole Church before the Father, that his will may be done. And they have also shown that concepts of 'offering Christ' were originally intended to be a kind of short-hand for the action of memorial itself in the Church.[5] On the other hand, the reaction against such piety by the Reformers themselves was not guaranteed to be an entirely balanced affair, not least when one takes into consideration that their knowledge of Christian origins, so dear to their hearts, was not as extensive as is ours today. To take two examples, it can only be a cause for regret that the *Didache* and the *Apostolic Tradition* of Hippolytus – and other documents from first few centuries – were either lost or not yet identified at the time of the Reformation when they could have served as useful theological cooling-systems in the heat of controversy. It is to their work, and the Anglican part of it specifically, that we must now turn.

II

A doctrine adapted, not rejected

In real terms, what did this adjustment at the Reformation amount to?

The Anglican Prayer Books betray a circumspect approach to this whole area. The 1662 eucharist, for example, directs that bread and wine be placed on the holy table, without any words to accompany the action, allowing it to be interpreted either functionally, or functionally-symbolically. Then, the priest reads a prayer 'for the whole state of Christ's church, militant here in earth', implying that it is only a prayer for the living, although there is a thanksgiving for the departed at the end, and near the start God is asked to 'receive these prayers, which we offer (sic!) unto thy Divine Majesty' (I Tim 2.1ff.). After the invitation, confession, absolution and the comfortable words, the thanksgiving follows, drawing the action of the Church into union with the angels and archangels. The prayer of humble access, on behalf of all the communicants, precedes the prayer of consecration, in the course of which the eucharist is expressed as 'a perpetual memory of that his precious death and passion, until his coming again' (I Cor 11.23–26). After the distribution of communion, the Lord's Prayer leads into the post-communion prayer, the first of which asks God 'mercifully to accept our sacrifice of praise and thanksgiving' (Ps 116.15), in which 'we offer and present unto thee, O Lord, ourselves, our souls and bodies, to be a reasonable, holy, and lively sacrifice unto thee' (Rom 12.1).

The first Prayer Books, of 1549 and 1552, however, bear the unmistakable imprint of the language and thought of Archbishop Thomas Cranmer (1489–1556). In Book V of his Answer to Stephen Gardiner (c.1495–1555), Bishop of

Winchester, on the eucharist, Cranmer expresses the same
key-reservations of the Reformers about the Roman Catholic
mass that lie behind his liturgy. It is worth quoting his main
principles, not just because they are typical of the time, but
because they come from him:

> '... Christ with once offering hath made perfect for ever them
> that be sanctified, putting their sins clean out of God's
> remembrance.'
> 'And that sacrifice was of such force, that it was no need to
> renew it ...'
> 'And that all men may better understand the sacrifice of
> Christ, which he made for the great benefits of all men, it is
> necessary to know the distinction and diversity of sacrifices.'

He goes on to distinguish between Christ's sacrifice, once and
for all, and those of the Church, which are 'made of them
that be reconciled by Christ, to testify our duties unto God,
and to shew ourselves thankful unto him. And therefore they
be called sacrifices of laud, praise, and thanksgiving.'
   And he proceeds to describe this eucharistic sacrifice in the
context of worship and life; that lay people participate in it
in exactly the same way as the priest; and that this was the
primitive understanding of sacrifice among the early
Fathers.[6]
   The Reformers may have lacked some of the knowledge of
the institutions and practices of the ancient Church that the
discoveries and recoveries of the past century have brought to
light. But they were learned in the writings of Augustine,
John Chrysostom, Eusebius, and their ilk. This gave many of
them (though not all, it has to be admitted) a constructively
critical perspective on their Catholic inheritance. William
Perkins (1558–1602), perhaps the most influential theologian among the early Puritans, taught at Christ's College,
Cambridge, and left behind a distinguished body of writings.
Critical of the need for everyone always to rely on a set form
of liturgy, and anxious to make the celebration of the eucharist more like a meal, with a dramatic breaking of the bread

and pouring of the wine, he was nonetheless fully aware of the rich theological tradition of the early centuries. And like many of the later Puritans, he advocated frequent eucharists, in the face of those who he thought neglected the sacrament. In an important passage, he defines his own understanding of how the eucharist is a sacrifice:

> The supper of the Lord is called a true and full sacrifice, not in that Christ himself is therein substantially offered, but it is true, both in the truth of representation and truth of the effect of the sacrifice of the cross which we obtain in the Communion, and likewise it is called true because therein the Church doth truly offer herself unto God, and also because it is the figure of the truth, i.e. of Christ offered, whome the sacrifices of the Old Testament did shadow.[7]

One can see behind these words a conviction to conserve, to explain, and to adapt, a tendency which we shall encounter again and again. The importance of Perkins lies in the fact that this process was already so well-tuned within a strand of Anglicanism that put a dual pressure on the Church both to loosen up the liturgy and to enrich its eucharistic theology. This was in time to result, at the Restoration, in some of their enthusiasts moving – or being moved! – into Nonconformity, a prominent example being Richard Baxter (1615–1691).

Central to the story, however, is the Prayer Book itself, often the base from which interpretation and reinterpretation arose. Three centuries on from Cranmer and Perkins, the Archbishops of Canterbury and York gave an *Answer* to Pope Leo XIII's *Bull* condemning Anglican Orders. At one stage, the *Answer* deals with eucharistic theology. It is interesting to see how it was possible to point to the powerfully sacrificial character of the Prayer Book eucharist without for a moment betraying the Reformation protest against the less desirable aspects of the mediaeval mass:

> We continue a perpetual memory of the previous death of Christ, who is our Advocate with the Father and the propitiation for our sins, according to His precept, until His com-

2-fold sacrifice

ing again. For first we offer the sacrifice of praise and thanks-giving: then we plead and represent before the Father the sacrifice of the cross, and by it we confidently entreat remission of sins and all other benefits of the Lord's Passion for all the whole Church; and lastly we offer the sacrifice of ourselves to the Creator of all things which we have already signified by the oblations of his creatures. This whole action, in which the people has necessarily to take its part with the Priest, we are accustomed to call the Eucharistic sacrifice.[8]

Not every Anglican Prayer Book followed this pattern exactly, and one of the features of Anglicanism – particularly in the twentieth century – has been the tendency for each Province to produce their own service-books.[9] As we shall see, many of these revisions move in quite surprising directions, including the introduction of offertory prayers, and forms of prayer at the consecration that offer the gifts in memory of Christ's death, along lines remarkably similar to the forms used in the Christian East. But for now, we must take note of this Anglican 'coolness' over offering-language. It is still there, it has not been expunged altogether, it is almost as if the very notion of offering is so adhesive to the essence of the Christian gospel that it is impossible to obliterate it from the eucharistic vocabulary.

There are a number of reasons which continue to make this theme topical in our own time, two of which stand out as of particular significance. One is the ecumenical rapprochement between the Churches, where so much headway has been made. Another, equally important, is the sheer fact that sacrifice refuses to die as an explanation of reality, as Frances Young has shown in relation to contemporary literature, for example in William Golding's *Lord of the Flies*, a novel in which a group of school-boys are washed up on a desert island without any grown-ups, an idyllic setting eventually turned into a scene of violence, in which one boy is killed as the 'scape-goat' of their ills.[10] Rather than try to justify how adhesive is the character of sacrifice to the eucharist in terms of its mere survival, I want to look instead at an important

(and neglected) contribution to the debate made by Leslie
Houlden in a collection of essays by members of the Church
of England Doctrine Commission in 1972, at a time when the
ferment in liturgical revision was really beginning in
earnest.[11]

Houlden begins with a discussion of the overall theme of
sacrifice, and then looks at the principal ways in which it
finds expression in the eucharist. (We shall be using three of
these, with some adaptation, later on.) With characteristic
fairness, Houlden describes them in terms of their background, and shows how some have stood the test of time (the
sacrifice of praise) while others (offering Christ's body and
blood) continue to be controversial. At the end of the essay,
Houlden makes two crucial points, one positive, the other
negative.

The positive point is his explanation of why sacrifice has
any importance at all:

> 'Chiefly, 'sacrifice' has one property which other images lack
> and which needs to be included in any account of the
> believer's relationship with God: totality of self-offering ...
> this remains its most useful feature, for how else can man
> come before God except in the attitude of sacrifice and with
> the intention to offer all?'

Houlden's negative point results from his discussion of just
how sacrifice can be expressed in the liturgy. For, he notes:

> 'One of the difficulties with most of the commonest formula-
> tions involving sacrificial language is that they start too far up
> the conceptual ladder; that is, they presuppose more funda-
> mental theological concepts which seem not to be fully clear,
> like a mountain whose summit is exposed while the lower
> levels are shrouded in mist.'

Behind these words lie almost a mirror of the reticence noted
earlier in the Prayer Book eucharist. The sacrificial aroma permeates the eucharistic table, for even in very provision of the
elements of bread and wine are to be seen the fruits of death
and life, of corn and grapes crushed and baked/fermented

into a new existence. And yet exactly how this aroma is described and reflected upon deserves careful attention. Every Western Church since the Reformation, including the Roman Catholic Church, has made important contributions to this open discussion. The Eastern Churches, however, have managed to hold a better balance, because of the richness and antiquity of their theological reflections as well as their prayers in the liturgy. Anglicans have long felt able, along with many others, to look at issues of importance from a wide perspective of history and antiquity.

III

Cross and Altar

We began with the Prayer Book. Before we tackle the more detailed discussions of Anglican theologians, it is appropriate to look first at a few of the <u>historic poe</u>ts of the tradition. This will serve to underline further the reticence and ambiguity of sacrifice in the tradition.

We start with John Donne (1571?–1631), one of the most striking and densely expressed of all our writers. In his famous poem 'The Cross'[12] we gain a vivid picture of the isolation of the crucified Christ, and the response of faith by the believer in the saving benefits of the eucharist. The language is rich, but the movement of ideas extraordinarily simple:

> Since Christ embraced the Cross itself, dare I
> His image, th'image of His Cross deny?
> Would I have profit by the sacrifice
> And dare the chosen Altar to despise?
> It bore all other sins, but is it fit
> That it should bear the sin of scorning it?
> Who from the picture would avert his eye,
> How would he fly His pains, Who there did die?
> From me, no Pulpit, nor misgrounded law,
> Nor scandal taken, shall this Cross withdraw.
> It shall not, for it cannot; for the loss
> Of this Cross, were to me another Cross.
> Better were worse, for no affliction,
> No Cross is so extreme, as to have none.
> Who can blot out the Cross, which th'instrument
> Of God, dewed on me in the Sacrament? ...

Once again, there is a sense of reticence. All the sacrificial language piles up in order to express the meaning of the cross itself, but the power of that cross meets the believer by the

118

abandonment faced before that symbol of the world's redemption. There may be a little play of words in the use of 'image', Donne harking back to his Roman Catholic upbringing, with its crucifixes, but seeing here the 'image' of all reality, judged and corrected and restored. For Donne, the altar is the cross, and his response is his whole life and ministry – 'no Pulpit, no misgrounded law ...' And the quotation ends with an eloquent statement of the power and virtue of the eucharist, where the blood of Christ is likened to the dew of the morning, harbinger of the new day, with all its opportunities.

George Herbert (1593–1633) alludes to the eucharist in several of his poems, but, for our purposes, nowhere more arrestingly than in the following stanzas of 'The Banquet':[13]

Welcome sweet and sacred cheer,
    Welcome deare;
With me, in me, live and dwell:
For Thy neatnesse passeth sight,
    Thy delight
Passeth tongue to taste or tell.

O what sweetnesse from the bowl
    Fills my soul,
Such as is, and makes divine!
Is some starre (fled from the sphere)
    Melted there,
As we sugar melt in wine?

Or hath sweetnesse in the bread
    Made a head
To subdue the smell of sinne,
Flowers, and gummes, and powders giving
    All their living,
Lest the enemy should winne?

Doubtless neither starre nor flower
    Hath the power
Such a sweetness to impart:
Onely God, who gives perfumes,
    Flesh assumes,
And with it perfumes my heart.

> But as Pomanders and wood
>   Still are good,
> Yet being bruis'd are better scented;
> God, to show how farre His love
>   Could improve,
> Here, as broken, is presented.

Herbert weaves into his ruminations the central themes of creation and redemption as these are to be discerned in the eucharist. Indeed, one can see perhaps most eloquently of all a determination to draw these together into a unity, in which the created order is turned into a vehicle of redemption itself: bread and wine, created from corn and grape, like the wood of the cross, and the penitent heart of the believer, who thereby experiences renewal of faith and life.

Another seventeenth century writer is Thomas Traherne (c.1636–1674), like Herbert a country parson, but, unlike him, largely unpublished until this century.[14] In his perhaps most famous work, the *Centuries of Meditations*, he writes in an almost ecstatic vein about the cross, often with eucharistic allusions or resonances, such as in the following:

> Had the Cross been twenty millions of ages further, it had still been equally near, nor is it possible to remove it, for it is with all distances in my understanding, and though it be removed many thousand-millions of ages more is as clearly seen and apprehended. This soul for which Thou diedst, I desire to know more perfectly, O my Saviour, that I may praise Thee for it, and believe it worthy, in its nature, to be an object of Thy love; though unworthy by reason of sin: and that I may use it in Thy service, and keep it pure to Thy glory.

Here we find the eternity of the cross, set within history, and reaching out to the believer through all the cultures and ways of life; and, most important of all, engendering a response of faith as already loved and redeemed. With an almost Augustinian sense of dependence on God, this meditation leaves the believer with something objective to grasp ('that I may use it in Thy service'), yet dwelling in human flesh ('and keep it pure to Thy glory'). It is hard to avoid the conclusion that Traherne is here, as elsewhere with his apostrophes to the cross, including the eucharist in the various ways in which the cross reaches out to people, only to evoke a response of faith, however stumbling.

Among his *Select Meditations*, there is one which extends and makes explicit what we have just glimpsed in the *Centuries*:

> Love is the only sacrifice. It is like our Saviour its own Priest and its own Altar. Perfume and flame. A Prophet Priest and King. O my God it is like thy Son, the Phoenix of the world. Its comprehensive sphere, a flaming Temple. The Antitype of her who is the feigned Miracle of all the Birds and more than so. Its own Altar fire nest and Sacrifice. O Thou Nest, and bed of Spices! In its Highest Agonies, ever Dying, Expiring and Reviving every moment.

It is not hard to see how Traherne, obscure writer as he can at times be, mingles his imagery within imaginable bounds. Love as the altar leads to new life, like the phoenix of legend, living again in a nest of sacrifice.

It is impossible to provide an adequate summary of how the poets of recent centuries have portrayed the eucharist in this general, allusive connection of altar and cross. One recent writer who has published some of his own poems is Rowan Williams. In a densely-packed meditation on the Rublev icon of the Old Testament Trinity,[15] he successfully conveys the movement of the three angels at the oaks at Mamre (Genesis 18), and the sacrificial provision of abundant fare for all:

> One day, God walked in, pale from the grey steppe,
> slit-eyed against the wind, and stopped,
> said, Colour me, breathe your blood into my mouth.
>
> I said, Here is the blood of all our people,
> these are their bruises, blue and purple,
> gold, brown, and pale green wash of death.
>
> These (god) are the chromatic pains of flesh,
> I said, I trust I make you blush,
> O I shall stain you with the scars of birth

> For ever, I shall root you in the wood,
> under the sun shall bake you bread
> of beechmast, never let you forth
>
> To the white desert, to the starving sand.
> But we shall sit and speak around
> one table, share one food, one earth.

This is perhaps the most explicit – in its allusive way! – that we have so far seen. God walks in from the outside, right into our environment, and wants to be identified with our life, which can only be done by taking on not only birth itself, but death, death wilfully inflicted young rather than expired through old age. Such an entry takes the form of entertainment to a meal, in which God's life is provided to human beings as sustenance for a journey far beyond the limits of usual life. To go further would do damage to the beauty of the poem, and if this paragraph has done damage, it would perhaps be better to read the poem again, and move on. Eucharistic sacrifice may be cool and reticent, but that does not mean that it has nothing to say in the new forms and experiences of the celebration as it moves into new ages, new cultures.

However, from these brief glances at some of the poets, we can sense both the possibilities and the limitations of seeing the eucharist as a sacrifice. If one gazes too intently on the cross, Christ becomes immobilised, and all the believer can do is surrender, nothing more. To nail Christ firmly to the cross is to deprive the eucharist of a vital part of its inner life. On the other hand, to invest too much in the celebration itself runs the contrary risk – of turning the cross into an overture to salvation, resulting in the individual celebration taking on the functions of the cross. What these poets help to remind us, as indeed does the Prayer Book rite, is that altar and cross stand in a relationship where altar feeds on cross, but altar is an action in its own right, a 'doing' in remembrance, in which time and eternity meet, and the Christian memory delved into, in order to make the past into the present and lead into the future.[16]

IV

Time and Eternity

Sacrifice, then, is an eternal reality that impinges on the Church, as it gathers in history. Before looking at how theological writers have discussed this relationship, it would be helpful bear in mind how the eucharist has been depicted in iconographic terms. When Jeremy Taylor (1613–1667) first wrote his *Worthy Communicant* in 1660[17], he included a frontispiece that expressed many of the aspirations of the Restoration Church, which he was able to inculate into the Church of Ireland, where he was a bishop. The reader looks at the interior of a gothic church building, with an east window in the distance. In the foreground stands the altar-table, with a reredos behind it. The altar is clothed with a frontal and there are rails on three sides for communicants to kneel. On the altar there are a chalice, chalice-cover (in the fashion of the time) and a large paten. But no one is there. Instead, two angels stand at either end of the altar, gazing at the table, behind which appears the text, 'Which things the angels desire to look into' (I Pet 1.12). Above, as if to summarise the whole scene, there is the face of another angel, with wings stretched out, a messenger from the heavenly places.

The sense of eternity in our midst is not a dimension of Anglican – or indeed other modern Western – worship high on today's priorities. And one may suspect that in Taylor's time, things were not that different. But in contemplating the eucharist, whether from the starting point of the presence of Christ, or of his sacrifice, we do not just stand in the here and now, but rather worship in the presence of a reality much bigger than ourselves. The perspectives of past, present, and future lie at the heart of the celebration, as the Prayer Book teaches when it describes the Lord's Supper as 'a perpetual memory of that his precious death, until his coming again'.

In order to bring out these three perspectives, we are now going to look at the eucharistic sacrifice from three points of view. They are, of course, inter-related. And when we refer to particular authors under one heading, this is not to imply that they were uninterested in either of the other two – though in a few instances this happens to be the case. The eucharist is, in the first instance, a memorial sacrifice, that looks back to the death of Christ. It is, in the second instance, a renewal of the covenant wrought by Christ and made accessible to believers now. It is, in the third instance, a union with the prayers of Christ at the Father's right hand, as we look to the future. Of course the cross is not just a past reality; indeed, that is why, for example, perspectives on the present and the future are necessary at all. Nor does the covenant exist exclusively in the present, for it looks back to the cross, and into the future. And Christ's priestly ministry in heaven results from the cross, and is available in the present. But, as we shall see, these categories when held together, demonstrate how rich the eucharistic sacrifice is, as a doctrine not rejected but adapted.

Do these approaches start – in Houlden's words – 'too far up the conceptual ladder'? To say that the eucharist is a memorial is only to state that it celebrates in some sense Christ's death. To renew a covenant is to express a corporate solidarity in the life of self-giving which God comes to share with his people. To join our celebration with Christ in heaven, in the figurative language of standing at the Father's right hand, is to say no more than that eucharist joins heaven and earth together.[18] Using perhaps the image of two people walking in opposite directions, Augustine wrote in Book XI of the *Confessions* that time 'must come out of the future, pass by the present, and go into the past; so it comes from what as yet does not exist, passes through that which lacks extension, and goes into that which is now non-existent.'[19]

However, the difference between time and eternity is not distance but difference. And, if we may adapt Augustine's analogy somewhat, the eucharist does not march from the future through the present into the past, but rather takes hold of the Church by emerging from the past and walking through the present into the future.

Anglican writers are not alone in trying to unravel the mystery of sacrifice, but they have their own contribution, and they keep addressing the issue from a number of vantage-points, whether in defending the Anglican position from attack (after the Reformation), or in order to bring some of the developing ideas into new liturgies (from the eighteenth century onwards), or with an ecumenical vision in which the kind of synthesis we shall be looking at has a constructive place alongside many others. Central, however, to the whole question of time and eternity is the place of memory, which Augustine explores in Book X of the *Confessions*, where he reveals a penetrating realism about the unconscious, and the need to 'bring together' different items in order to form a coherent whole.[20] Augustine's notion of memory was a profound influence on many of the founding fathers of Anglicanism, as, for example, in the case of Lancelot Andrewes (1555–1626), who was a prominent bishop in the reign of King James I. We shall be looking at his preaching in some detail later on. Memory and time stand behind so many of the characteristics of the Prayer Book, such as regular morning and evening prayer, the calendar and liturgical year, as well as the seasonal celebrations. The eucharist, embedded in the heart of the Prayer Book, cannot fail to be fed by such an approach, too.

V

A Memorial Sacrifice

No one denies that the eucharist is a celebration of the memorial of Christ's death (I Cor 11.23–26). The question is, in what sense? As we have seen, the question of sacrifice in relation to memory was controversial, helped by pastoral practice (which loomed, one suspects, larger in the Reformers' minds than some of the Catholic theologians) in which masses were repeatedly offered with few if any communicants. Something of the background can be seen in Lancelot Andrewes' *Responsio ad Apologiam Cardinalis Bellarmine* (1610), which was a work written at the behest of King James to answer criticisms made by Bellarmine, a prominent Catholic theologian and controversialist:

> Our men believe that the eucharist was instituted by the Lord for a memorial of Himself, even of His sacrifice, and, if it be lawful so to speak, to be a commemorative sacrifice, not only to be a sacrament and for spiritual nourishment. Though they allow this, yet they deny that either of these uses (thus instituted by the Lord together), can be derived from the other by man either because of the negligence of the people or because of the avarice of the priests. The sacrifice which is there is Eucharistic, of which sacrifice the law is that he who offers it is to partake of it, and that he partake by receiving and eating, as the Saviour ordered. For to partake by sharing in the prayer, that indeed is a fresh and novel way of partaking, much more even than the private Mass itself.[21]

[margin note: participation]

It is not hard to see the 'sub-text' of this passage. There can be no doubt, thinks Andrewes, that the eucharist is a commemorative sacrifice, and this is offered by all, not just the priest, hence the need for everyone to partake. It is not just a pastoral issue – he sees it as a theological question, because to celebrate the eucharist in such a way, whether because the people are lazy or because the priest is avaricious(!), that only the priest communicates is to set the priest apart in kind from the rest of the community. We are back to the gentle back-hander at the end of the Archbishops' reply to the Papal Bull against Anglican Orders: 'this whole action, in which the people has necessarily to take its part with the priest, we are accustomed to call the Eucharistic sacrifice.'[22] A cardinal aspect of this approach is to insist on receiving communion as an essential ingredient in the sacrifice.

But Andrewes was no fool, and was widely read in Catholic theology. Perhaps in a fit of oversimplification, he declares:

> Do you take away from the mass your transubstantiation; and there will not long be any strife with us about the sacrifice. Willingly we allow that a memory of the sacrifice is made there. That your Christ made of bread is sacrificed that we will never allow.[23]

Transubstantiation is the real problem, for the way in which it was taught at the time, the priest 'transubstantiates' the bread and wine into the Body and Blood of Christ at the words of institution in the eucharistic prayer. The result of such a notion was that the priest was then in a position to offer not the bread and wine of the eucharist, but the Body and Blood of Christ, in the memorial prayer (the 'anamnesis') which immediately follows in the liturgy. (This was probably one of the reasons for the Reformers' attachment to a eucharist rite that moved straight from the institution narrative to the distribution of communion itself.)

We shall be looking at Andrewes' sermons later on, as they are rich in numerous ways of looking at the sacrificial images through an imaginative exegesis of Scripture, particularly in the conclusions to his festival preachments, which often exhorted the congregation to make their communion.[24] Meanwhile, we can see something of Andrewes' wide-ranging approach to the eucharistic memorial through the fol-

lowing quotation from his *Preces Privatae* (Private Prayers).
These were for personal use during the celebration of the
eucharist This is how he prayed after the blessing:

> Finished and completed
> as much as lies in our power .
> CHRIST our God,
> is the mystery of your purpose and being.
> We have held the memory of your death
> we have seen the image of your resurrection
> we have been fed with your unending life
> we have been filled with your delights you possess
> so that in the world to come
> all of us may receive
> your blessing.[25]

A different theologian, but in the same school, was William
Laud (1573–1645), who died at the headsman's axe under
parliamentary pressure, having been a solid support to the
religious policies of Charles I. He took part in a conference
about the rights and wrongs of the Church of England held
in argument with John Fisher, a Roman Catholic in 1622.
The context, therefore, is not dissimilar to Andrewes' 'Responsio'. He has this to say:

> As Christ offered up Himself once for all, a full and all-suffi-
> cient sacrifice for the sin of the whole world, so did He insti-
> tute and command a memory of this sacrifice in a sacrament,
> even till His coming again. For at and in the Eucharist, we
> offer up to God three sacrifices: One by the priest only; that
> is the commemorative sacrifice of Christ's death, represented
> in bread broken and wine poured out. Another by the priest
> and the people jointly; and that is, the sacrifice of praise and
> thanksgiving for all the benefits and graces we receive by the
> precious death of Christ. The third, by every particular man
> for himself only; and that is, the sacrifice of every man's body
> and soul, to serve Him in both all the rest of his life, for this
> blessing thus bestowed on him. Now, thus far these dissent-
> ing Churches agree, that in the Eucharist there is a sacrifice of
> duty, and a sacrifice of praise, and a sacrifice of commemora-
> tion of Christ.[26]

Such a discussion immediately shows the limits of detailed analysis. Laud begins with an approach much in the mould of his mentor, Andrewes, which has allusions to the Prayer Book consecration. But he then seems to go beyond the parameters of a theology in harmony with the Prayer Book by delineating roles in the sacrifice. The priest prepares the bread and wine (and we may note the novelty of communion in both kinds, still having to be defended at the time), but this is done on behalf of the congregation. The second, truly, is offered by both – the commemoration itself. Why the third should be exclusively individual is hard to tell. It may be that Laud is trying to show the importance of the priest in the Anglican liturgy. It is true that some Anglicans have felt drawn to this kind of scheme, or something like it. But it does move in a new direction, and it also points up the consequences of definitions, both of detail and of role.

A more incisive mind was that of William Forbes (1585–1634) who taught at Aberdeen University for many years, before becoming, right at the end of his life, the first Bishop of Edinburgh. Unique among the seventeenth century writers, he travelled widely on the continent of Europe. In his (posthumous) *Considerationes Modestate et Pacificae* (= 'modest, peacemaking considerations' – an eirenical work on various aspects of controversy at the time), after quoting Andrewes on sacrifice not being such a problem if transubstantiation were forgotten, he admits that there is no explicit reference to the eucharist as a sacrifice in the bible. Yet he cannot let go entirely of something so deep in tradition:

> The holy Fathers say very often that in the Eucharist Christ's Body itself is offered and sacrificed, as appears from almost numberless places, but so, that not all the properties of a sacrifice are properly and really preserved; but by way of commemoration and representation of that which was performed once for all in that one only Sacrifice of the Cross, whereby Christ our High Priest consummated all other sacrifices, and by pious prayer; by which the ministers of the Church most humbly beseech God the father on account of the perpetual

> Victim of that one only Sacrifice, Which is seated in heaven on the right hand of the Father, and in an ineffable manner present on the holy table, that He would grant that the virtue and grace of this perpetual Victim may be efficacious and salutary to His Church for all the necessities of body and soul.[27]

This is perhaps the most balanced picture of the 're-offering' view of the eucharist, and it shows Forbes' deeply nuanced mind. It has a clarity which Laud lacks, and it always places the ultimate movement on God himself; all that we do is by way of response, in faith, yet that action is nonetheless a real and lasting one, for the eucharist requires human beings to perform it. Not all would agree with Forbes' approach, but it is useful to have a statement of one feature of the Catholic heritage in terms that are biblical and void of the heat of controversy.

The other main area of controversy, masses for the dead, is similarly dealt with by Forbes:

> The sacrifice which is performed in the Supper is not merely Eucharistic, but also in a sound sense propitiatory, and is profitable not only to very many of the living, but of the departed also.[28]

Forbes is not suggesting that the eucharist in some way appeases God's anger, or alters what is already done on Calvary. The centrality of the cross is abundantly clear from the earlier quotation. What he does seem to be saying is that the eucharist not only gives thanks for a past event, but supplicates God for the present and the future. Some would go no further than that, while others would accept the intercessory power of the eucharist, as a means of drawing together the living and the departed in the communion of saints. It is in the precise details of this relationship that many Anglicans continue to be reticent. Forbes may with some safety be regarded as the first self-consciously 'ecumenical' theologian in the Anglican tradition, because of the width of his personal contracts and his desire to probe into disputed areas in order to offer some kind of helpful synthesis.

Less open to such a Catholic-sounding view was Daniel Waterland (1683–1740), who worked along more conventional lines, basing his thinking on the Prayer Book rite and biblical categories:

> The service therefore of the Eucharist, on the foot of ancient Church language, is both a true and a proper sacrifice, ... and the noblest that we are capable of offering, when considered as comprehending under it many true and evangelical sacrifices: 1. The sacrifice of alms to the poor, and oblations to the Church; when religiously intended, and offered through Christ, is a Gospel sacrifice. Not that the material offering is a sacrifice to God, for it goes entirely to the use of man; but the service is what God accepts. 2. The sacrifice of prayer, from a pure heart, is evangelical incense. 3. The sacrifice of praise and thanksgiving to God the Father, through Christ Jesus our Lord, is another Gospel sacrifice. 4. The sacrifice of a penitent and contrite heart, even under the Law, (and now much more under the Gospel, when explicitly offered through Christ,) was a sacrifice of the new covenant: for the new covenant commenced from the time of the fall, and obtained under the law, but couched under shadows and figures. 5. The sacrifice of ourselves, our souls and bodies, is another Gospel sacrifice. 6. The offering up the mystical body of Christ, that is, his Church, is another Gospel sacrifice: or rather, it is coincident with the former; excepting that there persons are considered in their single capacity, and here collectively in a body ... 7. The offering up of true converts, or sincere penitents, to God, by their pastors, who have laboured successfully in the blessed work, is another very acceptable Gospel sacrifice. 8. The sacrifice of faith and hope, and self-humiliation, in commemorating the grand sacrifice and resting finally upon it, is another Gospel sacrifice, and eminently proper to the Eucharist.[29]

Waterland's approach reflects the Prayer Book liturgy, when he speaks of the offering of alms, oblations (presumably meaning the bread and the wine): the offering of prayer as sacrifice; the thanksgiving; the act of penitence itself; the offering of ourselves; the offering of the whole Church; the offering of converts and penitents (the evangelical and disciplinary features of the Church's work); and, finally, offering the commemoration of the sacrifice of Christ.

This is, indeed, an all-embracing scheme, and it has much in common with the approach to sacrifice that undergirds the eastern liturgies in its general approach, as if sacrifice were to be buttered right across the entire eucharistic celebration.[30] Apart from the two key areas of liturgy and biblical concept, Waterland's scheme relies heavily on that last form of offering – the memorial of Christ's one sacrifice. Indeed, one can see the way in which all the other notions of sacrifice rely on and lead up to 'the grand sacrifice', as a consequence of what he calls the 'Gospel' sacrifices. In other words, Calvary, though central, is to be seen in isolation neither from the Church's historic activity of worship and service, nor – by implication – from the whole life and ministry of Christ, which was so integral to Calvary itself. Many would welcome Waterland's specific approach to the memorial as more austere than Forbes or Laud. But Waterland's 'holistic' approach to the whole question is his real and lasting legacy to the debate. He works from the general to the particular[31] – a method that seldom fails to make theological headway when tackling a controversial subject.

Thomas Rattray (1684–1743) was like Forbes a Bishop in the Scottish Church, and like him also – but in a different way – a scholar of originality and flair. It is on his knowledge of the Eastern liturgies that the 1764 Scottish Communion Office largely relies, though his own eucharistic rite is more explicitly Eastern in its style and scope. What is of real and lasting interest is the way in which Rattray adopts an approach similar to Waterland's in his treatment of sacrifice. In the following quotation, we encounter for the first time the attempt (successful in the outcome) to change the liturgy in order to express a renewed and enriched theology of the eucharist. In both Rattray's own liturgy, and in the 1764 rite, the words of institution are a prelude not to the communion of the people but to the memorial prayer ('anamnesis'), with the offering of the gifts; a prayer for the descent of the Holy Spirit; followed by the general intercession for the living and departed. Rattray, like many others before him (including Andrewes and Forbes) knew of the way in which many of the Eastern eucharistic prayers handled these themes and he wanted to introduce them into his own Church. In his posthumous work, *Some Particular Instructions Concerning the Christian Covenant and the Mysteries by which it is Transacted and Maintained* (1748), he writes as follows:

> Then as Christ offered up His body and blood to God the Father under the symbols of bread and wine as a sacrifice to be slain on the cross for our redemption, so here the priest offereth up this bread and cup as the symbols of this sacrifice of His body and blood thus once offered up by Him, and thereby commemorateth it before God with thanksgiving; after which He prays that God would favourably accept this commemorative sacrifice by sending down upon it His Holy Spirit, that by His descent upon them He may make this bread and this cup ... as to be symbols or antitypes of the body and blood of Christ ... Then the priest maketh intercession in virtue of this sacrifice thus offered up in commemoration of, and in union with, the one great personal sacrifice of Christ, for the whole Catholic Church, and pleadeth the merits of this one sacrifice in behalf of all estates and conditions of men in it, offering this memorial thereof not for the living only but for the dead also, in commemoration of the Patriarchs, Prophets, Apostles, Martyrs, and of all the saints who have pleased God in their several generations from the beginning of the world; and for the rest, light, and peace, and a blessed resurrection, and a merciful trial in the day of the Lord to all the faithful departed.[32]

Rattray produces a more ambitious result from his understanding of eucharistic sacrifice than Waterland. But the similarities in method are nonetheless clear – move from the general to the particular, work through the liturgy as a whole, and ensure that everything stands in relation to Calvary. The new feature, occasioned by the prayer for the descent of the

Holy Spirit (commonly called the 'epiclesis'), is the Trinitarian focus of the whole prayer, a dimension sadly lacking in the Prayer Book rite. The general drift of the eucharistic 'argument' then takes on a new lease of life: narrate the institution, remember the work of Christ and offer the gifts of God, then pray for the descent of the Spirit as a consequence, and while praying for the gift of the Spirit, offer prayers for the whole Church, sealing the union of living and departed in Christ by this great act of prayer. In Rattray we can see something, too, of Forbes, with his determination not to undermine the centrality of the cross. What is offered is not the sacrifice, but its commemoration, in which the Church pleads the merits of that sacrifice. We shall return to the language of 'pleading' and the place of the Trinity again. Rattray, and others like him, pointed the way for the strengthening of eucharistic faith and practice under the Oxford Movement, which we shall look at when we discuss the heavenly offering of Christ.

More than a century later, however, after the Tractarian Movement's renewed emphasis on sacramental worship, Frederick Meyrick (1827–1906) wrote from an Evangelical standpoint about eucharistic theology. In a book that aimed to cover all aspects of the Lord's Supper, he demonstrates a thorough knowledge both of the early fathers and of the classical divines of the seventeenth and eighteenth centuries. What emerges is a carefully presented exposition of biblical and pastoral motifs.[33] In a different way, it has much in common with Waterland. He summarises the eucharist as being a remembrance, a sacrifice, a means of feeding, a means of incorporation, and a pledge. Of the first two he writes as follows:

> It is a Remembrance in so far as its object is to recall to the minds of Christians the love of Christ as exhibited in the sacrifice of His death; in so far as it commemorates by an outward act that Divine sacrifice; and in so far as it is a memorial of Christ and His death before man and before God.
> It is a Sacrifice, inasmuch as it is an offering made to God

as an act of religious worship – a *spiritual* sacrifice, as being
a sacrifice of prayer and praise to God for the benefits
received by the sacrifice of the death of Christ; a *material*
sacrifice, in so far as the bread and wine are regarded as gifts
of homage to God in acknowledgement of His creative and
sustaining power; a *commemorative* sacrifice, inasmuch as it
commemorates the great Sacrifice of the Cross – the words
'commemorative sacrifice' meaning, in this acceptation, a
commemoration of the sacrifice. But it is not a sacrifice of
Christ to His Father, whereby God is propitiated and man's
sins expiated.

From these two paragraphs one can see the close connection between remembrance and sacrifice, as well as a mildly
anti-catholic corrective at the end. The two themes stand
almost in parallel, as if Meyrick were trying to illuminate the
remembrance as a sacrifice, and the sacrifice as a remembrance. And when he discusses sacrifice, he opens the vista to
three approaches, spiritual worship, material offering, and
commemoration. But he ends his summary on the salutary
note that by combining remembrance, sacrifice, feeding, incorporation and pledge, 'we attain as nearly to a complete
notion and apprehension of it as the nature of a mystery will
admit.'[34] Somehow, that ending is worth waiting for.

William Bright (1824–1901) was a scholar of antiquity,
and he brings to our discussion both a ready sympathy with
tradition and a fidelity to Reformation sensitivities. In one of
this letters, he writes:

As for the sacrifice, I should begin by sweeping off the ground
all notions of a repetition of the atonement, of a new redemption, 'satisfaction', &c., so as to show that nothing like that is
intended.[35]

And in a frequently-used hymn, he works out this continuation of nuance and reticence which has appeared again and
again in our discussion in the following way:

And now, O Father, mindful of the love
That bought us, once for all, on Calvary's tree
And having with us him that pleads above,

we here present, we here spread forth to thee
That only Offering perfect in thine eyes,
The one true, pure, immortal sacrifice.

Look, Father, look on his anointed face,
And only look on us as found in him;
Look not on our misusings of thy grace,
Our prayer so languid, and our faith so dim:
For lo, between our sins and their reward
We set the Passion of thy Son our Lord.[36]

Such a hymn echoes at the outset the memorial-prayer
('anamnesis') of the early liturgies, and then moves on to
draw a contrast between the One Offering and the many
offerings, cross and altar. The language is carefully-phrased;
no sense of repetition, but rather 'spreading forth', a phrase
that resounds with the heavenly offering of Christ, which we
shall be looking at later. The hymn is proof of the enduring
quality of eucharistic poetry.

Can Meyrick and Bright agree? On essentials, yes. The language of memorial-sacrifice is strong in both, inescapable
even. Both rely on the once-and-for-all sacrifice of Christ.
Both invest the eucharist with a power that it would otherwise lack if the sacrificial aroma were not in the background
of the meal – that vital motif of total self-giving, which not
only describes the whole character of Christ's life and death,
but also points to the renewal of the believer in the life of
faith – including the forgiveness of sins. The difference, perhaps, is that Bright writes with a stronger devotional inten-
sity, which is not fully explained by the simple fact that he has
written a hymn and Meyrick has not. On the other hand,
Meyrick is clearly anxious to retain the character of sacrifice
not merely as a piece of doctrinal luggage, but as an essential
feature of the Lord's Supper.

Perhaps most germane to the twentieth century is the view
of memorial that has been popularised under the general
term 'celebration.' One name particularly associated with
this development is that of Gregory Dix (1901–1952).
Another scholar of antiquity, but perhaps with less sympathy

for the Reformation, he provides the following definition of memorial ('anamnesis') in his edition of the *Apostolic Tradition of Hippolytus*[37]:

> Words like 'memorial', 'remembrance', &c., have for us a connotation of a purely mental and subjective recollection of something in fact *absent*. 'anamnesis' has on the contrary the sense of bringing before God something which has happened in the past in such a way that its *consequences take effect in the present.*

Dix made this sort of statement repeatedly in his writings and is here expressing in a characteristically pronounced way an interpretation of early tradition that has found its place in contemporary ecumenical theology.[38] In one way, Dix was anticipated by some of the writers we have seen already, particularly by Andrewes, to whom we shall give special attention later on. Memorial is not just mental, it is an activity.

The real heart of the issue is about the concept of memorial, for it is from this foundation that everything else – whether it is offering alms, bread and wine, ourselves – is derived. In what sense is the eucharist a 'memorial' of the passion of Christ? We have seen various efforts to assert an active role for the eucharist. And some of them have started quite low down the conceptual ladder, including those which view the whole service – and indeed the whole of life, which it is supposed to echo – in sacrificial terms. We have also seen efforts to view the eucharist in Trinitarian terms, an activity of Father, Son and Spirit, in which the Son offers himself to the Father, from which offering the Spirit descends on the new creation. Modern eucharistic prayers frequently reflect some of these shifts since the Reformation era. They tend, however, to divide between those, like the Scottish-North American, in which the gifts of bread and wine are offered to God, and those, like the English-Australian, in which the memorial is made 'with this bread and this cup.'[39] What is the real difference, in historical and theological terms?

From an historical and theological point of view, there is

little doubt that in the earliest known prayer, the word used for 'offer' had soft undertones. In the Greek, 'prosphero' really means 'bring'. Indeed, one of the eucharistic prayers in the 1980 *Alternative Service Book* of the Church of England contains the words, 'we bring before you this bread and this cup.' The word has, in origin, no sacrificial action in mind other than the bringing forward of the gift, in preparation (cf. Mt 5.24). On the other hand, the more circumspect phrase, 'with this bread and this cup' places the emphasis more on the humanward action of God. But the two are not so far apart, in that they represent two key-movements: the presentation of the gifts for the blessing of God, and the making of the memorial before God with the gifts themselves as the obvious and essential context of the memorial.

At root, the 'memorial-sacrifice' looks back to the memory of the Church in God, in order to renew the life of faith in the life of Christ. Much of what we have seen has been a deliberate searching for treasures old and new (Mt 13.52), where writers in different contexts have looked to the past in order to reinterpret and adapt a doctrine of God's dealings with the whole of the created order in such a way that makes sense of its experience of trying to live that life of faith in the present. The memory has been both a resource for new ideas as well as the spur for the celebration to happen at all. But memorial-sacrifice is far from being the only motif, and it is now appropriate to look at our second 'time-set' way of seeing eucharistic sacrifice – the renewal of the covenant.

VI

A Covenant Renewal

One of the chief bible-texts for sacrifice is the self-oblation of *living sacrifice* the believer, the 'living sacrifice' (Rom 12.1). No one could disagree with this notion, thoroughly Pauline, and in line with the way in which sacrifice was 'spiritualised' in such a way that it went to the heart of the faithful person's response to the gracious and loving deity. From such a starting-point, it is not hard to make a connection with the eucharist, particularly in the language of covenant, which surrounds the accounts of the Last Supper (I Cor 11.23–26). Indeed, the language of covenant and sacrifice are so connected that it is at times hard to draw them apart.[40]

Self-oblation and covenant are two motifs that combine to *Exodus?* place a strong focus on the present reality of the eucharist. Memorial-sacrifice has to start with the memory of the past, and the heavenly offering inevitably draws the worshipper to the future. Thus, language which is at root concerned with the response of faith deals with the present reality in a way that is not so sharply-focused in the other two perspectives. Covenant is a theme that was used in antiquity, but it came into its own after the Reformation, precisely because of its biblical origins.

Before that, however, it is necessary to look at an approach that comes into covenant-renewal with something of a slant-movement. Because of the importance of the man in question, and his place in Anglican tradition, it would be a disservice to ignore him, not that anyone would want to.

Richard Hooker (1554–1600) was a scholar-priest who moved out of the limelight in order to write his *Laws of Ecclesiastical Polity*. In a startlingly original treatment of the sacraments, which comes tucked away only after dealing

139

covenant need – Exodus?

Hooker & covenant

with the Trinity and the Incarnation, he fastens on to a key-theme that leads towards covenant.[41] But he lays his ground carefully. In an eloquent passage, he comes to the heart of what the Christian is able to *do* in the response of faith. Conscious of the Reformation disputes about righteousness – whether it is 'imparted', as the Catholics maintained, and given directly to the faithful, or 'imputed', as Protestants maintained, and only made sense of through the cross – Hooker wrote as follows:

> We participate Christ partly by imputation, as when those things which he did and suffered for us are imputed unto us for righteousness; partly by habitual and real infusion, as when grace is inwardly bestowed while we are on earth.

In other words, Hooker is walking a prudent path, by maintaining (on the one hand) that the cross is central, but (on the other hand) that men and women still have a 'habitual' capacity for goodness – which he elsewhere describes as a 'first disposition towards future newness of life.' The implications for this for sacramental worship are not hard to see, particularly as these statements are set in the thick of his discussion of baptism and eucharist. Hooker wants to hold on to the eucharist as an activity of the Church, not a basking in the afterglow of Calvary. It happens *now*, not in the past, not in the mind, still less in the printed book. It thus engages with humanity, both in the innate capacity for good works, and in the redeemed life in Christ. This puts in mind a perceptive observation: 'Sacraments serve as the instruments of God ... moral instruments, the use whereof is in our hands, the effect in his.'

works & faith

In the eucharist, the Christian has a 'true and real participation of Christ', the effect of which is 'a real transmutation of our souls and bodies from sin to righteousness, from death and corruptibility to immortality and life.' ('Participation' is a word that he uses no fewer than ten times in his chapter on the eucharist.) The inward hold which unites the believer with Christ is a present reality. Hooker steers clear of direct sacrificial language, throwing the emphasis again and again on the present reality of the banquet, as in this quotation, coming at the end of his chapter on the eucharist:

> ... it serveth as well for a medicine, to heal our infirmities and purge our sins as for a sacrifice of thanksgiving.

He seems here to be using the term 'sacrifice of thanksgiving' in the sense of the eucharistic meal, which is central to his thought.

For future Anglican theology, Hooker was to prove a lasting influence. Because of the originality of his approach to 'participation', placing him somewhere in the scheme is not easy. But because of his important synthesis, with its stress on the 'now-ness' of the eucharist, we have chosen to make him a prelude to the more nuanced discussion of covenant as this evolved in the seventeenth century. It continued to be influential in the centuries afterwards, though in a more indirect manner.

Ralph Cudworth (1617–1688) was a Cambridge don who early on in his career wrote a treatise on the eucharist entitled *Discourse concerning the true Notion of the Lord's Supper.*[42] Here he set out to link the eucharist with the Jewish (and other traditional religious) custom of holding sacrificial meals, where the community 'feast upon things sacrificed.' It is perhaps one of the first attempts to view the eucharist in these terms and to argue for a direct relationship between the Passover meal and the eucharist in this way. This led him to the conclusion that the eucharist is not a sacrifice in the strict sense of the word, but a feast upon a sacrifice. Cudworth's knowledge of the Jewish literature is formidable. But it is not only there to probe into origins; he uses it to argue his case, which comes in the final chapter.

In it, he comes to the second main argument, that 'the eating of God's sacrifices was a federal rite, between God and those that offered them'. He recognises that this insight is not 'so vulgarly understood', but he makes a strong plea for the eucharist to be seen as a binding together of the worshippers *what covenant?-*

with one another and into covenant with their Lord. Moreover, he sees the eucharist as a renewal of this covenant. Covenant was a commonplace theological term at the Reformation.[43] By Cudworth's time, the danger was that it might be taken over and used by the more radical Puritans to express the relationship between God and his people in exclusive terms. This tendency is, as we all know, not just a feature of the seventeenth century religious scene. Nor is it entirely undesirable. One of the paradoxes of Christian living – and it goes right through all areas of ministry, from baptism policy to who is welcomed at the communion – is the fine balance between affection and demand, between making the gospel accessible to people, and ensuring that it is also sufficiently challenging. To err in one direction is to dilute it; to err in the other is to make it exclusive.

yes!

In terms of the time of writing, Cudworth's intention is probably threefold. First, he is using the tools of his trade, as a biblical scholar, to offer fresh insights into the origins of the eucharist – something which scholars of all ages make their own. Second, he wants to combat any notion of the eucharist as a sacrifice in the primary sense of the word – hence he latches on to the 'feast upon the sacrifice', the sacrifice being Calvary. Third, he wants to loosen up the increasingly popular theme of covenant in order to give it a God-human focus. If anything, there might be a temptation to make the eucharistic covenant an activity in which the human race are the key-players.

continual covenant renewal

Cudworth's style lacks the devotional aura of Hooker, but it has its own clarity and lightness:

> Now, therefore, that we may return; As the legal sacrifices, with the feasts upon those sacrifices, were federal rites between God and Men: in like manner I say the Lord's Supper under the Gospel, which we have already proved to be a feast upon sacrifice, must needs be a feast of amity and friendship, between God and men. Where by eating and drinking at God's own table, and of his meat, we are taken into a sacred covenant, and involiable league of friendship with him.[44]

Hooker's solidity of participation and the Cudworth's covenant-theology, with its human outworkings in friendship and bonding in faith, left their mark on many writers. Two deserve particular mention.

The first is Herbert Thorndike (1598–1672). Like Cudworth he was a University teacher, and he became a Canon of Westminster at the Restoration. His writings are verbose and overflowing with ideas. But there are some central themes, one of which is covenant.[45] Indeed, near the start of one of his major discussions of the eucharist, he writes:

> The celebration of the eucharist is the renewal of the covenant of grace. Is grace a covenant?

We enter the covenant at the font, and renew it at the Lord's Supper. And in a style reminiscent of Cudworth, he declares:

> Those that communicate in the eucharist do feast upon the sacrifice of our Lord Christ on the cross, which God is so well pleased with as to grant the covenant of grace, and the publication thereof, in consideration of it.

Sensitive to the centrality of the cross, he goes further:

> It is not nor can be any disparagement to the sacrifice of our Lord Jesus Christ upon the cross, to the full and perfect satisfaction and propitiation for the sins of the world which it hath made, that the eucharist should be counted the sacrifice of Christ crucified, mystically, and as in a sacrament, represented to, and feasted upon by, His people.

He goes on to elaborate the different aspects of sacrifice as these are found in the liturgy, in a manner we have seen already: the offertory, the intercession, the consecration, and after communion in the self-offering of the communicants. Of this he writes penetratingly:

> Hereupon arise a fourth reason, why this sacrament is a sacrifice; to wit, of the bodies and souls of them, who, having consecrated their goods to God for the celebration of it, do by receiving it profess to renew that consecration of themselves

> to the service of God according to the law of Christ, which
> their baptism originally pretendeth. For inasmuch as we
> revive and renew the first profession of our Christianity in
> receiving the eucharist, we do also, by the same means, 'offer
> up our bodies for a living sacrifice, holy and well pleasing to
> God, which is our reasonable service'; as St Paul com-
> mendeth, Rom. xii.1.

The other writer was perhaps more influenced by Cudworth.
Simon Patrick (1626–1707) was taught by him at Cam-
bridge, and via parochial appointments and the Deanery of
Peterborough became Bishop, first of Chichester and then
Ely. While still a parish priest, he wrote his *Mensa Mystica:
or a Discourse concerning the Sacrament of the Lord's
Supper*[46], which appeared in 1660, the year of the Restora-
tion, and the same year as the publication of Taylor's *Worthy
Communicant*.

Patrick's style is simple and down-to-earth. He summarises
the theology of the eucharist under various headings, taking
care to point out that:

> *anamnesis* doth not signify barely 'recordatio', recording or
> registering of his favours in our mind; but "commemoratio",
> a solemn declaration.
>   We keep it, as it were, and plead before him the sacrifice of
> his Son, which we show unto him, humbly requiring that
> grace and pardon, with all the other benefits of it, may be
> bestowed on us.

We shall come across the use of the word 'plead' again, noting its significance at this point as a key-word in the eucharistic vocabulary. He goes on to emphasise again that the
eucharist is not a mental affair:

> I would not be so mistaken, as if I thought the Christian
> thanksgiving consisted only of inward thoughts and outward
> words. For there are eucharistical actions also whereby we
> perform a most delightful sacrifice unto God ... The spiritual
> sacrifice of ourselves, and the corporal sacrifice of our goods
> to him, may teach the papists that we are sacrificers as well as
> they ...

7.

Echoing Cudworth, Patrick describes the eating and drinking of the bread and wine as 'a federal rite' and 'a feast upon a sacrifice'. 'Our approach to this table is but more strongly to tie the knot, and to bind us in deeper promises to continual friendship with him.' Again and again, Patrick emphasises the serious character of the undertakings of sharing Holy Communion as an offering of ourselves to God, but he always gives an equal emphasis on the enjoyment that this sacred meal conveys by its essential character.

One can see in these two scholars slightly contrasting ways of adapting covenant-imagery. Like Thorndike, Patrick taught that we enter the covenant at baptism and renew it at the eucharist. Patrick has less to say, but his market was the wider Church, whereas Thorndike wrote for the intelligentsia. Both have at the back of their minds the Prayer Book rite – another important aspect of Anglican tradition which continues in our own time in the somewhat different liturgical scene before us.

Before we move on into a different era, it is appropriate to evaluate where we have got to in relation to this covenant-renewal approach to the eucharist. In Hooker, we saw the key-term 'participation' and it formed the basis for his understanding of the eucharist as present reality. Then in Cudworth, the 'covenant' theme is brought out of Scripture and applied to the eucharist as an expression of solidarity with each other and God. Then Thorndike and Patrick, in different ways, use this approach not only to draw a contrast between cross and altar, but to express the sheer delight of being at the eucharist – a theme Patrick repeats again and again. Delight and pleasure are present realities that the Church should expect to experience as the covenant is renewed.

Perspectives inevitably shift with the passing years, but we have laid these foundations for the covenant-view because they keep resurfacing in new guises. Two centuries on, F.D. Maurice (1805–1872), perhaps one of the most original minds in the Anglican theological scene, wrote his *Kingdom of Christ*,[47] a defence of the Prayer Book and its underlying theology and ecclesiastical position. In a different world, he offers an approach that has much in common with what we have so far seen:

> When we say that our feast, like that of the Passover, is sacrificial, we do not mean that it does not commemorate a blessing which has been fully obtained and realized; if we did we should violate the analogy in the very moment of applying it; for the Passover did commemorate a complete deliverance and the establishment of a national state in consequence of that deliverance. But as that deliverance was accompanied with a sacrificial act, and by a sacrificial act accomplished, – and yet in this Passover the act was perpetually renewed, – because in this way the nation understood that by sacrifice it subsisted and consisted, – and because by such a renewal its members realized the permanent and living character of the good that had been bestowed upon them, so it is here.

And he proceeds:

> The sacrifice of Christ is that with which alone God can be satisfied and in the sight of which alone He can contemplate our race; it is therefore the only meeting-point of communion with Him; but this communion being established, it must be by presenting the finished sacrifice before God that we both bear witness what our position is and realize the glory of it; otherwise we have a name without a reality, and with the words 'finished and completed' are robbing ourselves of the very thing which makes it so important that we should prize them and preserve them.

In the first quotation, Maurice provides us with the analogy of the Passover and its renewal for the people who have been shaped by it. It is in some ways a more reflective way than Patrick's, breathing even more an experiential approach. But it is in the second quotation (which follows immediately in Maurice's text) that we come across the theological gold. Christ is the means of our communion with the Father, which means that in the eucharist we must fulfil our celebration by 'presenting the finished sacrifice before God'. And he goes on to imply that if we refrain from celebrating the eucharist (which is the practice of some of those he has in mind in writing his book, who were Quakers) 'we have a name without a reality', in other words, the potential for claiming access to God without the action that expresses it. There is something, too, of the 'delight' we saw earlier when Maurice speaks not only of bearing witness to the sacrifice but realising the glory of it, hence the need to prize, cherish and value it.

William Temple (1881–1944), who was much-influenced by Maurice, takes a similarly wide approach in one of his most famous works, *Christus Veritas*.[48] Working along lines that are by now familiar, he writes:

> The divine life offered in the Eucharist is the life of the divine love (expressed in uttermost self-sacrifice – Body broken, Blood shed) of which the human counterpart is universal fellowship.

And later on:

> The sacrifice of Christ is potentially but most really the sacrifice of Humanity. Our task is, by His Spirit, to take our place in that sacrifice. In the strict sense there is only one sacrifice – the obedience of the Son to the Father, and of Humanity to the Father in the Son. This was manifest in actual achievement on Calvary; it is represented in the breaking of the Bread; it is reproduced in our self-dedication and resultant service; it is consummated in the final coming of the Kingdom.

Then:

> The Eucharist is a sacrifice; but we do not offer it; Christ offers it; and we, responding to his act, take our parts or shares in His one sacrifice as members of His Body.

What we have here are three fundamental truths, each of which stands firmly on the foundation of the ultimate definition of sacrifice, totality of self-giving. First, the bread and wine are in themselves signs of costly fellowship. Second, our response to the sacrifice of Christ is renewed obedience in faith, which is why Christ's obedience is 'represented' in the eucharist. Third, the response is about being members of His Body, to live that life of costly self-giving.

Rowan Williams, whom we have already quoted as a poet, falls into a similar mould when he writes about the eucharist. In a study of what he calls the 'metaphor' of eucharistic sacrifice,[49] he ends his historical comments on origins with a heartfelt plea for this 'solidarity' at the Lord's table. Incapable of any superficial chumminess, Williams writes with a God-centred passion that has much to commend it:

> The whole of our worshipping activity is an expression of the reconciliation in the mortal flesh of Christ between God and his creatures. We bring ourselves near to the altar of the cross as we come and offer our gifts – and we are encouraged to do so because the way is open through the flesh of Christ – and are brought to the Father as we claim the fruition of the covenant proclaimed in the paschal event. Through the Spirit's work, the covenant is 'renewed' in us, in our re-entry into the "sanctuary" of Calvary.

And, again, in his book *Resurrection*, a study of the theology of Easter[50], he draws attention to the 'easter-character' of every eucharist, not only as a joyful ending to the passion, but as a prelude to yet more costly living of the life of faith:

> If the risen Jesus is present where men and women turn to their victims and receive back their lost hearts, then he is 'materially' present where this process involves a specific material transformation – where the effective significance of material things is changed.
>
> As has been said, the Christian Eucharist provides the central interpretative model for this: our food and drink is given up into the hands of Jesus so that we become his guests and receive our life from him. The elements are shifted from one context of meaning to another, from being our possessions to being gifts given and received back ... But this transaction does not occur exclusively in the Eucharist – and indeed its 'occurrence' in the Eucharist in isolation from its occurrence

in the Christian community's life is ... a gross offence against the true significance of the sacrament. It occurs whenever we make the essential transition from seeing the material world as possession to seeing it as gift: as God's gift to us, and as, potentially, a gift to be given and received between human beings.

There is, of course, far more than covenant-renewal behind these eloquent lines, but that is the central theme, and perhaps this is what makes the renewal of christian life so central to the 'present' reality of the eucharist. For here is Hooker's dynamic 'participation', Cudworth's 'federal rite', Thorndike's renewal in grace, Patrick's delightful sacrifice before God, Maurice's means of communion with God, Temple's finding our right place within the sacrifice of Christ, and Williams' challenge to go forth and *live* the life of God.

This is where time and eternity meet again – as the present moves out of the past and proceeds in weak human flesh into the future. As far as conceptual ladders go, the advantage of the broadly 'covenant' approach is that it draws together many more clusters of experience than at first sight appears. But, then, that need hardly surprise, given the fact that its primary focus is on the present. When the followers of Christ are told to 'do this', they respond by doing it! What covenant brings above all is that dimension of cost – but also delight. But if it lives a life detached from Calvary, it takes on its own specific agendas that are always less than the Kingdom of God, and when left in isolation from the future, it lacks direction. As Methodists have shown in their own way with the annual service of renewal of covenant, this approach to Christian living needs more than one outlet in celebration.[51] It could be, however, that a renewed emphasis on the covenant aspect of the eucharist might offset the perhaps disproportionate enthusiasm in certain quarters for baptismal renewal rites. Once again, therefore, eternity can feed the collective memory by continually existing in time.

Where do all these themes find their place in the liturgy?

the most obvious focus in the Prayer Book rite is where 'we offer our souls and bodies' after receiving communion; or, in the adjacent prayer, in which we ask for grace, 'that we may continue in that holy fellowship, and do all such good works as thou hast prepared for us to walk in.' Both these themes, the explicit self-offering, and the prayer for grace to live faithfully, continue in the revised liturgies. They are, too, implicit in the other gestures of costly fellowship, for example the reintroduction of the peace, and the dismissal – which is not an announcement, but a command. And they are, too, features of the Prayer Book Exhortations before Holy Communion, which are usually skipped over, and which have no modern counterpart.[52] Sometimes when they occur in new post-communion prayers, they read rather easily, belying the gunpowder so carefully wrapped up in cotton-wool, as with the following, taken from the American *Book of Common Prayer* (1979):

> Eternal God, heavenly Father,
> you have graciously accepted us as living members
> of your Son our Saviour Jesus Christ,
> and you have fed us with spiritual food
> in the Sacrament of his Body and Blood.
> Send us now into the world in peace,
> and grant us strength and courage
> to love and serve you
> with gladness and singleness of heart;
> through Christ our Lord.[53]

VII

A Heavenly Offering

The intercession of Christ at the Father's right hand (Hebrews 7.23–25) as part of our story is beset with ironies. First of all, of our three main perspectives, it has the least foundation in the Prayer Book communion rite, though it has to be said that the Collect for Ascension Day, based as it is on the mediaeval Latin original, does take us in that direction.[54] This should hardly surprise, however, given the nature of the festival:

> Grant, we beseech thee, Almighty God, that like as we do believe thy only-begotten Son our Lord Jesus Christ to have ascended into the heavens; so we may also in heart and mind continually dwell, who liveth and reigneth with thee and the Holy Ghost, one God, world without end.

The second irony is that this theme should be so prominent a feature in Calvin's theology, as several people have recently pointed out.[55] Indeed it would almost seem that Calvin's eucharistic theology relies more on the place of Christ in heaven, interceding for humanity, than on memorial or renewal of covenant, strong as these two approaches appear in his writings.

The third irony is perhaps a consequence of this, that the heavenly intercession holds a prominent place in contemporary ecumenical agreement, as we shall see. For when we tackle the 'heavenly offering', we are speaking about what *Christ* does in and through the Church in a way that is not so explicit in memorial and covenant-renewal.

The fourth irony is that this theme has been adopted in various ways by a number of Anglican (and other) theologians

151

as a starting-point, and it has yielded great fruit, for its sheer power and beauty.

However, the fifth irony takes us back to Houlden's conceptual ladder, for this approach starts at a higher level than either memorial or covenant. With both the former two approaches, there are immediate analogies from human experience, as well as direct accessibility of terms. A memorial-offering and a renewal of a binding agreement are not exactly everyday terms, but they have a directness that few would be able to challenge. Not so with Christ in heaven. This may be partly because the union of earth and heaven is an aspect of worship in general and eucharist in particular that is not high on the agendas of Christians today. It may also be because the climate of our times mistrusts the imagination: pictures have to have an obvious meaning, news-bulletins have to have summaries that are easy to understand, and if the meaning of something does not leap immediately to the understanding then it is discarded.

I exaggerate in order to make a point, which is that whether the image of Christ praying at God's right hand is the correct way or not, there has to be some means of placing the eucharist in a context beyond the here and now, otherwise it would become locked into the present, looking back to the past. And if we simply think of the future of our race and our world and no more, the whole dimension of the kingdom of God becomes limited – a very un-New Testament attitude. By opting for this image, we are saying that God listens to us, through Jesus Christ – as so many ordinary prayers conclude. And this listening capacity is part of God's nature – for he can do no other. The Prayer Book Collect for the twelfth Sunday after Trinity, also based on a mediaeval original, puts this succinctly:

> Almighty and everlasting God, who art always more ready to hear than we to pray …

To place the eucharist in this context of God's readiness is to interprose cross between God and eucharistic altar. The question is, how can this image live a life of its own, circumscribed by reasonable disciplines, and ensure that the 'future' dimensions of eucharistic faith and practice breathe and expand?

Jeremy Taylor, whom we have mentioned already in connection with his *Worthy Communicant* (1660), is perhaps one of the pioneers of this approach as H R. McAdoo demonstrates in his detailed study of Taylor's eucharistic theology. Like Simon Patrick's *Mensa Mystica*, Taylor's work begins with a theological statement of what the eucharist is about, and then leads on to practical considerations. Taylor's is a subtle mind, ready to weave together different ideas, for he lacks the plainness of Patrick. Among the blessings and graces of Communion he includes the following.[56] It is a famous passage, and it is worth quoting at length:

It is the greatest solemnity of prayer, the most powerful liturgy and means of impetration in this world. For when Christ was consecrated on the cross and became our high-priest, having reconciled us to God by the death of the cross, he became infinitely gracious in the eyes of God, and was admitted to the celestial and eternal priesthood in heaven; where in the virtue of the cross He intercedes for us, and represents an eternal sacrifice in the heavens on our behalf. That He is a priest in heaven, appears in the large discourses and direct affirmatives of St Paul; that there is no other sacrifice to be offered but that on the cross, it is evident, because 'He hath but once appeared in the end of the world to put away sin by the sacrifice of Himself;' and therefore since it is necessary that he hath something to offer so long as he is a priest, and there is no other sacrifice but that of Himself offered upon the cross; it follows that Christ in heaven perpetually offers and represents that sacrifice to His heavenly Father, and in virtue of that obtains all good things for His Church.

Now what Christ does in heaven, He hath commanded us to do on earth, that is, to represent His death, to commemorate this sacrifice, by humble prayer and thankful record; and by faithful manifestations and joyful eucharist to lay it before the eyes of our heavenly Father, so ministering in His priesthood, and doing according to His commandment and His example; the church being the image of heaven, the priest the minister of Christ; the holy table being a copy of the celestial altar, and the eternal sacrifice of the lamb slain from the beginning of the world being always the same; it bleeds no more after the finishing of it on the cross; but it is wonderfully represented in heaven, and graciously represented here; by Christ's action there, by His commandment here.

We are, in one sense, on familiar ground, because as with memorial, there is a careful balance to be kept between what was done once and for all, and what the Church does as part of that eternal act of God. Taylor's flowery language delights in repetition, but his meaning is seldom unclear. Relying on the Letter to the Hebrews (Heb 7.24, 8.3), he then links this heavenly ministry specifically with the eucharist; Christ is in heaven, and eucharist becomes an extension of his prayer for us, hence the image of the earthly table being a copy of the eternal altar in the heavenly places. Such language, once decoded, means no more than that the eucharistic celebration has an eternal dimension because it is part of Christ's offering of himself to the Father the result of which is the fulfilment of Christ's promises – 'all good things for His Church.' As Taylor a little later on says[57]:

> It is an intercession for the whole church present and absent, in the virtue of that sacrifice ... It is all but the representment of His death, in the way of prayer and interpellation, Christ as head, and we as members; He as high-priest, and we as servants His ministers; and therefore I shall stop there, and leave the rest for wonder and eucharist.

When someone as eloquent as Taylor deliberately refrains from going further, the reader senses that we are in the presence of something mysterious, transcendent, and beyond words, the mystery of sacrifice. It is no wonder, therefore, the the heavenly offering is not only attractive to Taylor, but encompasses areas of eucharistic piety that would otherwise be lacking. And it brings to the fore two essential movements, union with Christ, and prayer for the eucharist as part of the

Church's *future.* For the conjoining of these two aspirations provides for the eucharist the vital dimensions of divine objectivity and human conditionedness. It would easy to give these broad, heavenly horizons a needless sacramental triumphalism, which would, in any case, be far from Taylor's own heart. The union of the earthly and the heavenly, and the present with the future, is precisely to claim for the eucharist a place in the redemption of the world in God's ways, and in God's time. Perhaps more than any other writer, Taylor weaves out of this approach not a self-conscious balance, but a paradox – a paradox in which God is active not merely in the Church as a historical community, but in the whole world, the terrain of his loving purposes for *all*.

A cooler variant of this approach is to be found in Daniel Brevint (1616–1695), a Channel Islander who, *via* exile in Paris during the Commonwealth, became a prominent figure at the Restoration, and eventually Dean of Lincoln. In his *Christian Sacrament and Sacrifice* (1673) he sets his whole theology of the eucharist around eternal Christ's sacrifice, which replace the sacrifices of the Old Testament, and which Christians celebrate in the eucharist as a memorial, and in union with Christ's prayer in heaven[58]:

> This victim having been offered up both in the fulness of time and in the midst of the habitable world, which properly is Christ's great temple, and thence being carried up to heaven, which is his proper sanctuary, thence he spreads all about us salvation, as the burnt offering did its smoke, as the golden altar did its perfumes, and as the burning candlestick its lights. And thus Christ's body and blood have every where, but especially at the holy communion, a most true and *real presence.* When he offered himself upon earth, the vapour of his atonement went up and darkened the very sun; and by rending the great veil, it clearly shewed He had made a way to heaven.
>
> Now since He is gone up to heaven, thence he sends down on earth the graces that spring continually both from his everlasting Sacrifice, and from the continual intercessions which attend it. So that it is in vain to say, *who will go up into*

> *heaven*? since, without either ascending or descending, this
> sacred body of Jesus fills with atonement and blessing the
> remotest parts of this temple.

Brevint's style is more succinct and more biblical. He uses
Old Testament imagery and then depicts Christ's death,
whereas Taylor assumes it has happened. But it is the same
basic message, the union of the earthly and heavenly, as in the
following passage:

> For Jesus Christ and his Church so concur together in one
> oblation, that the blessed Saviour contributes all that can go
> up to heaven to please and appease God; and we, on our part,
> do contribute but what deserves to be removed out of the
> way, the corruption and smell of sin.

Behind this language there stand two special sensitivities.
First, Brevint is conscious of sinful humanity, in need of forgiveness, and unworthy to approach God; second, he is con-
fident that in spite of this, God is still prepared to give us
grace and strength. For Brevint, the eucharist's prime purpose
is to seal the forgiveness of sin, and thus point the believer
towards future newness of life. His importance is enhanced
by the strong influence he had on John and Charles Wesley,
sons of Epworth Rectory, not far from Lincoln, to whom we
shall be giving some attention later.[59]

Edward Bickersteth (1786–1850) takes us on into a later
era. His *Treatise on the Lord's Supper*, published in 1824 and
republished subsequently in abbreviated devotional form,
reflects Evangelical sensitivities about the all-sufficiency of
the cross, which must not be undermined by giving the
eucharist a life and force independent of that One Sacrifice.[60]
But he allows the eucharist a Godward direction:

> This is done for our own edification, as a testimony to the
> world, and as a prevailing mode of pleading merits before
> God. It has been observed that 'What we more compen-
> diously express in that general conclusion of our prayers,
> *through Jesus Christ our Lord*, we more fully and forcibly
> represent in the celebration of the Holy Eucharist, wherein we

plead the virtue and merits of the same sacrifice here, that our Great High Priest is continually urging for us in heaven'.

This perhaps takes us back to the basic starting-point of the heavenly offering, prayer to the Father through Christ. Moreover, Bickersteth uses the word 'plead' here twice, and he does so on other occasions. We saw it in Simon Patrick's *Mensa Mystica*, and we shall see it again, from Anglicans of various traditions. It suits particularly well as a liturgical expression of the heavenly-futurist direction of the eucharist. But the all-sufficiency of the cross kept being reasserted. Nathaniel Dimock (1825–1909) was a prolific author, learned in the early Fathers and sensitive to Reformation principles, who on one occasion cautioned that 'with this Sacrifice (i.e. Christ's) in full view of our faith, with this as the object of our remembrance, we want nothing more. Nay, we can see that there is room for nothing more.'[61]

Alexander Jolly (1796–1838) was a Scottish Bishop who lived at a time when it was necessary both to defend the Scottish Communion Office of 1764 and to assert the community of faith between the Scottish Episcopal Church and the Church of England. In his great work, *The Christian Sacrifice in the Eucharist* (1831), which stands in the same tradition of Taylor's *Worthy Communicant* and Patrick's *Mensa Mystica* as both devotional and theological in style and intent, he holds out for the memorial-sacrifice as real and effectual, and concludes his seminal discussion with the following:

> Meantime, following Him, we shall not walk in darkness, but have the light of life. As long as this lower world shall endure, and the time of trial for salvation last – until death, the last enemy de destroyed, He ever lives, in his mediatorial capacity, to make intercession for us, and bring us to God. In the highest heavens, He presents the substance of His Body and Blood once offered and slain upon earth, and which must in heaven remain until the time of the restitution of all things; and His Church upon earth by the hands of those He com-

missioned and promised to be with them, in succession of His Apostles, to the end of the world, offers the instituted representations of them in commemorative sacrifice, to plead the merit and pray for all the benefits of His death and Passion, pardon of sins, increase of grace, and pledge of glory.

Upon this memorial, of his Son's appointment, the Father ever looks with propitious eyes; and that bread and wine may become channels of such inestimable blessings, sends down His Holy Spirit to enliven and invigorate the outward signs, to such a degree, that they may be, not in substance, which is in heaven only, nor merely in figure or representation, but in effect and full virtue, the body and blood of His Son, to all intents and purposes of our salvation.[62]

Here we have a carefully nuanced timescale of pardon of sins (the past), increase of grace (the present), and pledge of glory (the future), repeated themes in Jolly's work, as well as a firm belief in the union of eternal sacrifice in heaven with historical eucharist on earth, and a gentle repudiation of transubstantiation. The legacy of Taylor lives on, as Christ's 'substantial' body is located in heaven, while not for one moment diminishing the power, force and virtue of his presence through the eucharist on earth.

Our last two examples are Robert Wilberforce (1802–1854), an Oxford scholar who eventually became a Roman Catholic, and Richard Parsons (1882–1948), a theologian who became Bishop of Southwark, and then of Hereford. It is interesting to note how both are drawn to the heavenly offering of Christ as an indispensable way of expressing the eucharist's action and movement.

Wilberforce, in his *Doctrine of the Holy Eucharist* (1853), relies on the imagery of Hebrews in a way by now familiar:

The Holy Eucharist, therefore, is fitly called the Christian Sacrifice, not only because it is the chief rite of common worship, but because it is the peculiar act, wherein the effectual intercession, which is exercised in heaven by the Church's Head, reaches down to this lower sphere of our earthly service.

And he proceeds:

> Such is the principle upon which the Holy Eucharist is called a sacrifice. It rests upon the necessity of Our Lord's Intercession: upon the truth that the Church's services cannot be effectual, unless they are presented by its Head: that His intervention is essential, not only because He communicates grace to His members, but because His members cannot be accepted save through the sacrifice of Himself.[63]

Like John Henry Newman (1801–1890), in his Anglican days, and Edward Pusey (1800–1882), Wilberforce used the term 'pleading the merits of that sacrifice', in an earlier work on the incarnation. Pusey, in a sermon preached in 1836, could say that 'we plead the death of His Son, and in that we plead it, we are accepted.'[64] The word 'plead' we have now encountered in a number of writers, and it would appear to have a wide degree of trust and acceptance. McAdoo uses it as a way of summarising Taylor's theology.[65]

Richard Parsons, as Bishop of Southwark, was anxious to provide a unitive approach to understandings of the eucharist at a time of dissension between the various strands of Anglicans in his diocese. In 1936 he carried out a 'Primary Visitation' to Southwark clergy, in which he spoke about eucharistic doctrine. Later that year, it was published under the title, *The Sacrament of Sacrifice*, and appended with a hymn by Parsons himself, in order to express the main theological motifs of his discussion. Central to his treatment is the unity of heaven and earth, and the dynamic of the relationship between the two:

> The sacred Feast is itself a consummation of His sacrifice manwards, as the heavenly Session is its consummation godwards. It is offered by God to man, it is offered by man to God; the Priest and the Victim are one and the same, Jesus Christ, Himself true God and true man. In the unchanging activity of His one and inadvisable Person he offers Himself in perfect love as God to man and as man to God. The true altar, in the deepest and most real sense, is the Heart of Jesus Himself. In its infinite love this Heart enclosed every faithful

heart in all the ages which communiates with Him in his self-
giving love to God and man. Upon that divine yet human
altar on high the fire of love is ever burning. Through the
sacrament which He has ordained His self-offering is made
present to His people on earth, so that they may make it
theirs, and be offered with Him in the corporate oblation of
the Body of Christ, which is His Church, one, holy, catholic,
apostolic, visible and invisible, militant and triumphant.[66]

One can see between these lines some of the old sensitivities,
and, perhaps, the influence of Temple, to whom Parsons
served as Suffragan Bishop of Middleton at Manchester some
years earlier. The language has a directness and a pastoral
warmth. The theology is rooted in what has emerged as a
sound tradition, in which the One sacrifice is central and
eternal, the many offerings historic and human, but only performed because of that Single Sacrifice, to which it stands
united.

Something of these sentiments come across in the hymn
Parsons wrote, the first verse of which is as follows:

We hail Thy Presence glorious,
O Christ our great High Priest,
O'er sin and death victorious
At Thy thanksgiving feast;
As Thou art interceding
For us in heaven above,
Thy Church on earth is pleading
Thy perfect work of love.[67]

We began our discussion of this particular approach urging a
basic defence, in the face of its absence from the Prayer Book
eucharist, and the complexity of its imagery. And we may
note in passing increasing references to Christ 'our great
High Priest' in modern liturgies. We showed that, as a logical
result of prayer 'through Christ', the eucharist is celebrated
in and through his place with the Father, whether that 'place'
is interpreted as intercession, pleading – or 'sitting', as in
many Eastern liturgies. In a sense, these latter categories are

important, for even though all liturgical and doctrinal language is analogical, to *equate* the Church's prayer with Christ's would do damage to the character of both. To speak of Christ praying to the Father for us is to say no more than than that he is 'with us always, to the close of the age' (Mt 28.20). We do not need to use the elaborate language of Taylor, or the biblical exotics of Brevint, in order to regard the eucharist as a heavenly offering. In this respect, some of the more restrained language of more recent writers, including Bickersteth and Parsons, sustains the Hebrews imagery, but makes it more accessible.

But there are two more fundamental reasons why this approach is so important. We have cited the Letter to the Hebrews on a number of occasions so far. In one passage, which we have not yet cited, the writer contrasts Christ's sacrifice with those of the Law, and goes on to speak of its *effect*:

> For if the sprinkling of defiled persons with the blood of goats and bulls and with the ashes of a heifer sanctifies for the purification of the flesh, how much more shall the blood of Christ, who through the eternal Spirit offered himself without blemish to God, purify your conscience from dead works to serve the living God. (Heb 9.13f)

The two features of this text which make the heavenly offering no mere option but essential to a full understanding of the eucharist are the role of the Spirit and the gift of the Spirit in the *future* of the Church. To 'plead' Christ's sacrifice is to 'remember' it before God. But it means more than that, for it means moving on from there and inviting the Spirit into the life and heart of the Church – not that the Spirit was absent in the first place. To pray the eucharistic prayer is to be in love with the future. To plead the merits of Christ's death is to be open to the Spirit's workings and to pray for all manner of concerns, general and specific, as part of that single, flowing action of prayer around the table of sacrifice.

Something of this is to be found in a passage from Augustine's *City of God*, which would have been familiar to many – if not all – the writers looked at thus far. In Book Ten, when discussing sacrifice in relation to worship and living, and in the context of a world in which many beliefs lived side-by-side, Augustine provides a short, pungent chapter which – if given an added dose of the Holy Spirit – sums up much of what we have been saying:

> Wherefore the true mediator, being in the form of a servant, made mediator between God and man, the man Christ Jesus, taking sacrifices with his Father, as God, yet in the servile form chose rather to be one than to take any, lest some hereby should gather that one might sacrifice unto creatures. By this is He the priest, offering, and offerer.
>
> 'The true sacrament whereof is the Church's daily sacrifice: which being the body of Him the Head, learns to offer itself by Him. The ancient sacrifices of the saints were all divers types of this also, this being figured in many and divers, as one thing is told in many words, that it might be commended without tediousness. And to this great and true sacrifice, all false ones gave place.[68]

VIII

The Unbloody Sacrifice[69]

There is one blanket-term which appears in eucharistic discourse from time to time that deserves passing mention. In the Testament of the Twelve Patriarchs (probably late second century BC), the true and pure worship offered to God is referred to as 'reasonable and unbloody' – reasonable because it is spiritual, unbloody because it does not involve the slaughter of any animals. Such a description started being used of the Eucharist in the East, where it still appears in the eucharistic liturgy. Medieval Catholic theologians use it from time to time, in order to make a distinction between the One Sacrifice of Christ, and the many offerings of the Church, but it never caught on in mediaeval liturgies. Perhaps this is because it might have seemed to imply something less than what was in due course called 'transubstantiation', i.e. because of its obvious stress on the cereal nature of the eucharistic of bread. Some of the Reformers were happy with it as a description of the eucharist, precisely because of its implied distinction between Christ's offering and ours, including John Jewel (1522–1571), the prominent Elizabethan theologian, in his controversies with the Catholic Thomas Harding.[70] Simon Patrick uses it in the *Mensa Mystica*, also drawing on Origen's description of the 'unsmoky sacrifice', i.e. one that does not burn! And John Johnson (1662–1725), Vicar of Cranbrook in Kent, wrote a lengthy tome in two parts on eucharistic theology awesomely entitled *The Unbloody Sacrifice*. Although it never enters official Anglican liturgy, it stays on the sidelines, and one suspects two reasons for this.

The first is the obvious one, the sheer starkness of the term

163

[handwritten margin note: Y Lord did it have to?]

itself as a 'summing up' of what the whole eucharist is about.
The second reason is that the term 'unbloody' makes the necessary contrasts, but does not dwell in any one of the main
categories of approach we have used up to now, i.e. memorial, covenant, or heavenly offering. In fact, it resembles more
the kind of imprecise, reticent language of 'cross and altar'.
In his important book, *The Body of Christ*, Charles Gore
(1853–1932) gives a powerful all-embracing description of
the eucharistic offering in the following typical paragraph:

> But all this language of disparagement of material sacrifices
> still leaves them on their own ground recognizing that the
> worship in spirit and in truth is not a mere inward and indi-
> vidual approach to God, but a corporate and therefore out-
> ward thing – a worship which publicly acknowledges God in
> all His gifts, though He needs them not; and a worship that
> finds central expression in the eucharist, in which, according
> to the ordinance of Christ, bread and wine are presented to
> the Father, in the name of the Son, and in memorial of His
> passion, with the adoration and prayer and thanksgiving of
> sons, and blessed by the Holy Spirit to become the Lord's
> body and blood, and partaken by the worshippers that they
> may be bound all together in Him. That was for the
> Christians the chief and central expression of rational service
> and bloodless sacrifice.[71]

One can see the various strands coming together, the memorial, the covenant, the heavenly offering; all more than just
mental recollections of a personal kind, and merging into
worship that is reasonable and unbloody.

There is one aspect, however, of the 'unbloody sacrifice'
which deserves more than passing mention. It will be remembered that in the Prayer Book communion rite, the bread and
wine are placed on the holy table, without prayer. And this
was a special point of reticence at the Reformation, because
of the overlay of mediaeval offertory prayers in the days of
the old Latin mass. The 'unbloody sacrifice' makes the point
that it is not human flesh that is being sacrificed, but bread
and wine being sanctified for a holy use.

[handwritten margin note: grain offering]

In the period since, some of the revisions of the liturgy have reintroduced offertory prayers, usually of a 'down-beat' nature. Indeed, the prayers used in the 1970 Roman Catholic Missal with their focus on *God* as the giver of all good things ('through *your* goodness we have this bread/wine to offer ...') have appeared in some Anglican rites. On the other hand, there are some liturgies which resolutely refuse to say anything at the presentation of the gifts, since that detracts from the eucharistic prayer.[72] What bearing does this have on our discussion?

It is true that with the passing of the years, many Anglicans have lost their fear of 'offering gifts', particularly when they look to the East and see ancient imprecision surviving, and reformed Roman Catholic worship in which some of the excesses of the past have been corrected. However, there will still be Anglicans who are averse to offertory prayers, except when offering money, one of the main innovations when the first Prayer Book was issued in 1549. Practice does differ quite markedly; for example, in North America, there are no prayers at the presentation of the bread and wine in the USA, whereas in Canada there are optional prayers, which vary (along with the Collect and Post-Communion prayers), though they normally use all-embracing language, such as 'receive all we offer you this day'.[73] Is this ambiguity in fact an ambivalence? To be sure, it is hard to make neat distinctions over which prayer refers to money and which to bread and wine, especially when both categories – and sometimes yet more! – are presented at the altar around the same stage in the eucharist. Rowan Williams sums up the general position in an neat aside in the course of his book, *Resurrection*:

> ... in spite of a proper caution about speaking too loosely of the elements being "offered" to God in the Eucharist, we still need to say that the moment of *relinquishing what is ours* is crucial in the eucharistic process.[74]

All this amounts to is simply this: the 'unbloody sacrifice' is spiritual and material, and in an age in which ecological concerns loom far more largely than they could have done four centuries ago, there may well be a place for offertory prayers, or prayers presenting the gifts to God, provided that it is made clear that God is the ultimate giver of all, and that we are only giving back to him what is his already (I Chronicles 19.11–14).

IX

Two case-studies:
1. Lancelot Andrewes

One of the pitfalls of adopting a method in order to describe what is a complex reality, is that not everything will fit neatly into the compartments that are provided for the purpose. We have already seen how in each of the three main approaches, memorial, covenant, and heavenly offering, not every writer has entirely fitted. The purpose of these two case-studies is to demonstrate this truth even further. We begin with Lancelot Andrewes' preaching.

Sermons are not doctrinal treatises (like Hooker's *Laws*), nor are they theological-devotional manuals (like Taylor's *Worthy Communicant*), nor yet are they attempts at providing unifying approaches at a time of controversy (like Parsons' *Sacrament of Sacrifice*). When a particular preacher addresses a congregation year by year at the major festivals, and uses the text for the sermon in countless ways, *including* the call to receive communion at the end, then we should not be surprised if we found that the eucharist is made to fit into just about any theme. Such a course of action may not make the best systematic theology, but it has a cumulatively powerful effect on the faith and practice (we hope!) of the listeners. Andrewes' preaching moves around in many directions, and the following examples will show just how diversely the eucharist can be interpreted in a sacrificial sense.[75]

First, preaching on the second commandment at St Giles' Cripplegate in January 1592, he draws together sacrament and sacrifice:

> For many among us fancy only a Sacrament in this action,
> and look strange at the mention of a Sacrifice: whereas, we
> not only use it, as a nourishment spiritual (as, that is too) but
> as a mean also, to renew a covenant with God, by virtue of
> that sacrifice, as a Psalmist speaketh (Ps 50.5). So our Saviour
> Christ in the institution, telleth us, Luke 22.10, and the
> Apostle, Hebrews 13.10. And the old writers use no less, the
> word Sacrifice, than Sacrament; Altar, than Table; offer, than
> eat; but both indifferently, to shew there is both.

Then there is a cluster of small references: at Christmas
(1610) the eucharist is a thank-offering for the glorious birth.
On Easter Day, 1617, preaching on the 'sign of Jonas' (Mt
12.39f), he declares that the eucharist is for 'the raising of our
bodies out of the dust of death.' On Low Sunday in 1600, on
the forgiveness of sins (Jn 20.23), he lists the ways in which
this can be known, starting with baptism, and going on to the
eucharist. On Christmas Day (1616), preaching about the
meeting of the virtues (Ps 85.21), he applies these virtues to
Christian living, as transformed by the eucharist ('the sooner
and the better to procure this meeting, the Church meets us
... with bread and wine'). The following year, on Christmas
Day, preaching on Lk 2.12f, he waxes rhetorical on the weak,
poor elements, offering life and sustenance to all ('for Christ
in the Sacrament is not unlike Christ in the cratch (i.e. crib)')
and he likens the feast to a sacrifice of praise.

At Whitsun (1610), he turns his text (Jn 14.15f) into a
covenant-renewal in the eucharist towards the conclusion:

> To a covenant, there is nothing more requisite, than to put the
> seal. And we know the Sacrament is the seal of the new
> Covenant, as it was of the old. Thus by undertaking the duty
> He requireth, we are entitled to the comfort which here He
> promiseth. And, do this, He would have us, as is plain by His
> *hoc facite* (= 'do this').

At Christmas (1620), preaching on the wise men from the
east (Mt 2.1f), he asserts that the way to keep the festival is
to celebrate the Saviour's memory: 'by the offering, breaking,

and partaking of which body, we are all sanctified, so many as shall come to it. For, given it is, for the taking away of our sins.' And at Easter (1609), with the greeting of peace as the text (Jn 20.19) he likens the eucharist to the peace-offering, urging his hearers to partake of it, as the Jews did of old.

Finally, preaching at Easter (1612) on I Cor 5.7f ('cleanse out the old leaven'), Andrewes works out a full statement of his eucharistic theology. Christ is the sacrifice, the passover, the feast. 'If Christ be a propitiatory sacrifice, a peace-offering, I see not how we can avoid, but the flesh of our peace-offering must be eaten in this feast by us, or else we evacuate the offering utterly, and lose the fruit of it.' Moreover, it is a remembrance and a receiving (he uses the Greek words 'anamnesis' and 'katalepsis'), both together. But the remembrance is an action, not just words. 'It is not mental thinking, or verbal speaking: there must be actually somewhat done, to celebrate this memory'. But the sacrifice is eternal (Christ's) and historical (the eucharist). With an almost Augustinian focus on time and eternity, Andrewes says that 'that sacrifice (was) but once actually performed, at His death: but ever before represented, in figure, from the beginning; and ever since repeated, in memory, to the world's end. That only absolute; all else relative to it, representative of it, operative by it.'

Time and eternity join together by a juxtaposition of movement:

> And we are, in this action, not only carried up to Christ (*sursum corda*, i.e., 'lift up your hearts') but, we are also carried back, to Christ; as he was at the very instant, and in the very act of His offering. So, and no otherwise, doth this text teach. So, and no otherwise, do we represent Him. By the very incomprehensible power of His eternal Spirit, not He alone, but he, as at the very act of His offering, is made present to us, and we incorporate into His death, and invested in the benefit of it ...

And just before the end, Andrewes applies this time-motif:

> There is a further matter yet behind: for as this feast looketh back, as a memorial of that, is already past and done for us: so doth it forward, and is to us a pledge of another, and a better yet to come, the feast of the marriage of the Lamb here, that is our passover: where, whosoever shall be a guest, the angels pronounce him happy and blessed for ever.

There is much that could be said of all this. Andrewes' prose is better sipped than gulped. But it is clear from these choice-quotations that his mind is alert to the need for vivid portrayal of the eucharist within the seasonal terms of each occasion. He can throw the eucharist into any important corner of the biblical world and still ensure that it returns intact, enriched by a new context, even when it is most surprising, but invariably still untouched in any way that would detract from its inner meaning and divine life. For Andrewes, there is no single understanding of the eucharistic sacrifice. We have seen cross and altar; memorial; covenant; heavenly offering; and we have also glimpsed at the 'unbloody' sacrifice in his treatment of the elements of bread and wine. And yet all the time, he walks circumspectly over Reformation sensitivities, ensuring that Christ's death is central, shedding light on this sacrament for which Andrewes seems to have a never-ending repertoire of images and pictures. In our own very different world, we would do well to preach so imaginatively.

X

Two case-studies:
2. John and Charles Wesley

In 1744, the year after his death, Thomas Rattray's liturgy was published, an event that was to bear fruit in the centuries to come, with its clear signals of interest in the Eastern eucharistic prayers, hence its stress on the role of the Spirit in the new creation. We are still living with the legacy of his work. In the following year, an equally significant event took place in the form of the publication by John and Charles Wesley's *Hymns on the Lord's Supper*.[76]

Although the path which John Wesley eventually took led him away from the Church of England, these hymns were written while he was still firmly within its fold. In any case, the hymns are the property of the whole Church Catholic and their intrinsic interest lies in two important aspects. The first is that when they were first published, the Wesley brothers (and we may assume that Charles was the prominent mind here) prefixed the collection with an abridged version of Daniel Brevint's *Christian Sacrament and Sacrifice*.[77] As was pointed out earlier, the Wesley brothers were brought up in Epworth Rectory, not far from Lincoln, where Brevint had been Dean towards the end of his life. His reputation would have outlived him. In any case, the way in which these hymns are set out owes a great deal to Brevint's writing, which includes the general approach taken with sacrifice.

The second factor which tends to be overlooked is the very reason why these hymns were written. Of course, we have been told repeatedly that 'Methodism was born in song.' And there are no hymns in the Prayer Book, except if one allows

the hymn to the Holy Spirit in the ordinal. The sheer importance of sacred song must not be overlooked. But what of the
context of the hymns? They were written to be used in conjunction with the Prayer Book eucharist. It is not beyond the
bounds of possibility that they were composed – at least in
part – to *supplement* a rite which *lacked* some important
notions about the eucharist. In other words, we are in a
world not that far removed from Rattray, the liturgy-writer.
Anglicanism is moving on, and that means debate, tension,
synthesis.

The hymns are divided into six sections: memorial, a sign
and means of grace, a pledge of heaven, the eucharist as it
implies a sacrifice, the sacrifice of our persons, and after the
sacrament. It is worth quoting a few of these hymns in full,
to illustrate what he has to say. We shall be looking at one
from each of the sections concerned with sacrifice.

First on memorial:

1

Then let us go, and take,
  and eat
The heavenly, everlasting
  meat,
For fainting souls prepared;
Fed with the living Bread
  Divine,
Discern we in the sacred
  sign
The body of the Lord.

2

The instruments that bruised
  Him so
Were broke and scatter'd
  long ago,
The flames extinguish'd were;
But Jesu's death is ever new,
He whom in ages past
  they slew
Doth still as slain appear.

3

Th' oblation sends as sweet
  a smell,
Even now it pleases God
  as well
As when it first was made;
The blood doth now as freely
  flow,
As when His side received the
  blow
That show'd him newly dead.

4

Then let our faith adore
  the Lamb
To-day as yesterday the
  same,
In Thy great offering join,
Partake the sacrificial food,
And eat Thy flesh and drink
  Thy blood,
And live for ever Thine.

There is a great deal here that is by now familiar. The One Sacrifice, the many eucharists; the single self-offering of Christ, the feast upon that sacrifice; eternal event, historical celebration; and, perhaps most significant of all, the pouring in of the divine life, to be with God for ever.

Then, as 'implying a sacrifice':

1

Live, our Eternal Priest
By men and angels blest!
Jesus Christ the Crucified,
He who did for us atone,
From the cross where once
    He died,
Now He up to heaven
    is gone.

2

He ever lives, and prays,
For all the faithful race;
In the holiest place above
Sinners' Advocate He stands,
Pleads for us His dying love,
Shows for us His bleeding
    hands.

3

His body torn and rent
He doth to God present,
In that dear memorial shows
Isarel's chosen tribes imprest;
All our names the Father
    knows,
Reads them on our Aaron's
    breast.

4

He reads, while we beneath
Present our Saviour's death,
Do as Jesus bids us do,
Signify His flesh and blood,
Him in a memorial show,
Offer up the Lamb to God.

5

From this thrice hallow'd shade
Which Jesus's cross hath made,
Image of His sacrifice,
Never, never will we move,
Till with all His saints we rise,
Rise, and take our place above.

Once again, there are many motifs brought into this hymn: the high priest, the risen Lord, the union of the earthly and heavenly, the memorial-sacrifice, and the end of all things.

Finally, 'the sacrifice of our persons':

1

Let Him to whom we now
 belong
His sovereign right assert,
And take up every thankful
 song,
And every loving heart.

2

He justly claims us for His
 own
Who bought us with a price:
The Christian lives to Christ
 alone
To Christ alone he dies.

3

Jesu, Thine own at last
 receive;
Fulfil our heart's desire,
And let us to Thy glory
 live,
And in Thy cause expire.

4

Our souls and bodies we
 resign,
With joy we render Thee
Our all, no longer ours,
 but Thine
Through all eternity.

Self-offering is the dominant theme of this hymn: between its lines we can discern the renewal of covenant ('Our all, no longer ours, but Thine' is, surely, an echo of 'I am no longer my own ...' from the Covenant Service). Here is the faithful response to the gospel-sacrament.

Although the hymns are grouped by sections, nonetheless, one can see the way in which they mingle and relate to each other, rather life the preaching of Lancelot Andrewes. It is not possible to pin sacrifice down too closely. But thematic approaches do help towards a better understanding of the movement of different ideas. As we have already seen, the Wesley hymns are by no means the only ones. But they form an outstanding contribution, and have both expressed and fed eucharistic piety in all traditions, and in many different places.

XI

Two catalysts

It is now time to gather together the various threads of the past and look more specifically at the present. Before we do so, we draw attention to two catalysts in the eucharistic debate, both of them as it happens lay people. Earlier on, Gregory Dix's emphasis on memorial as a dynamic representation was described. That needs gentle highlighting now, as 'anamnesis' understood in comparable terms becomes significant as we enter the era of ecumenical convergence.

The first catalyst is Will Spens (1882–1962), a Cambridge don, who made an important contribution to *Essays Catholic and Critical* (1926).[78] He begins his discussion of eucharistic sacrifice with the following statement:

> If a student of comparative religion, not otherwise acquainted with Christianity, were to enter a church where the Holy Mysteries were being celebrated, and were afterwards asked what kind of service he had been attending, he would undoubtedly say that it was some sacrificial rite; and he would find his answer endorsed if he were to turn from the service which he had witnessed to the earliest narration of its institution.

And, more pungently still, towards the end:

> Further pleading of that death in the Eucharistic liturgies is valuable as bringing out what is thus involved. It can add nothing to what is involved.

We are now into an age that looks even more critically at Christian institutions. It is impossible, therefore, to pretend that the eucharist is not at root what other religions would interpret it to be. On the other hand, it is its own form of sacrifice, for it is in the pleading that its real character can emerge.

Second, Evelyn Underhill (1875–1941) made a significant but neglected contribution to the debate. We should, of course, note that this is the first woman-theologian mentioned so far, a harbinger, no doubt, of things yet to come.

In her all-embracing book, *Worship* (1936) she held fast to sacrifice as an indispensable aspect of the eucharist:

> It is strange, that the most painful of all the discussions and conflicts which have raged round the Eucharist, have centred on the extent, and sense, in which it can be regarded as a sacrifice.[79]

But she defines it in general terms, and has much in common with the many of the writers we have looked at so far, including Augustine. She goes to the heart of the matter in *The Mystery of Sacrifice* when she insists that sacrifice is not propitiating an angry God, but giving him an invitation:

> Here, the human creature presents his little offering, the raw material of his concrete yet symbolic sacrifice; and with this small gesture of generosity he moves out towards the Supernatural, goes up to the Altar of God, becomes part of the great spiritual action of the Church in Christ her Head, and is subdued to the movement of the whole.[80]

But an additional flavour to Underhill's writings – apart from a strong affirmation of the transcendent impinging on the thoughts and feelings of worshippers – is her stress on the role of the Spirit:

> This conviction of the direct personal action of the immanent Spirit of God on and in the praying Church, revealing to it the deep mysteries of Eternity, controlling its decisions and supporting its labours, is seen in its noblest form in the Pauline Epistles, and in its practical consequences in many passages of Acts.[81]

Indeed, so strong was this underlying sense of the presence

and work of the Spirit that a recent writer has termed Underhill's view of the eucharist as a 'pneumatological oblation.[82] At a time when there were moves to revise liturgies so that they could include this dimension, it comes as no surprise that Underhill, an enthusiast for Eastern prayer, should write in this way. But she is not interested in introducing new words for their own sake. She wants to get to the heart of the matter, hence the urgency with which she writes. Worship is about the contemplation of God – and flows into joyful service by a community of redeemed sinners. If the eucharist is about anything, it must be about that movement of offering.

almost a
dance metaphor

XII

Ecumenical Statements

When the Anglican-Methodist scheme for union failed to reach sufficient majorities in the Church of England in the late 1960's, a group of Evangelicals and Anglo-Catholics put forward an alternative set of proposals, which contained an appendix called 'eucharistic sacrifice – some interim agreement'. We have seen thus far how differing strands of Anglicans view the eucharist as a sacrifice, and so it is appropriate that this particular document should be quoted, not only for its own merits, but because of the intra-Anglican ecumenism which it espouses:

> What, then, do we offer at the Eucharist? Christ offered himself on the cross in our stead and without our aid, and we certainly cannot repeat that offering. We do, on the other hand, offer not merely 'the fruit of the lips'; not merely undefined 'spiritual sacrifices'; not merely ourselves, considered apart from Christ; not even ourselves in Christ if that is seen in separation from our feeding on Christ; but ourselves as reappropriated by Christ.[83]

Here we find common ground, that allows the eucharist an autonomy, but places it in the heart of Christ's activity for his world.

Of far more significance, however, was the Anglican-Roman Catholic International Commission's 'Statement' on eucharistic doctrine (1971). Fastening on to the notion of 'anamnesis' as dynamic memorial, the 'Statement' goes on to give the eucharist that autonomy, and it is interesting to note in the following quotation the three main approaches outlined earlier, namely memorial, covenant, and heavenly offering of intercession:

> In the eucharistic prayer the church continues to make a perpetual memorial of Christ's death, and his members, united with God and one another, give thanks for all his mercies, entreat the benefits of his passion on behalf of the whole Church, participate in these benefits and enter into the movement of his self-offering.[84]

What is the Ch/?

Remarkable as this converge is, it nonetheless leaves open the question of exactly *how* the eucharist does enter into that self-offering. Modern Anglican liturgies often lack the cool reticence of the Prayer Book, though this is reflected in the Church of Ireland's eucharistic prayer (1984):

> Therefore, Father, with this bread and this cup
> we do as Christ your Son commanded:
> we remember his passion and death,
> we celebrate his resurrection and ascension,
> and we look for the coming of his kingdom.
> Accept through him this our sacrifice
> of praise and thanksgiving ...[85]

On the other hand, the Scottish Liturgy (1982) goes further, both offering the gifts and uniting the eucharist with Christ's eternal sacrifice:

> We now obey your Son's command.
> We recall his blessed passion and death,
> his glorious resurrection and ascension:
> and we look for the coming of his Kingdom.
> Made one with him, we offer you these gifts
> and with them ourselves,
> a single, holy, living sacrifice.[86]

what are these gifts!

But neither text contradicts the ARCIC 'Statement'. What has happened over the years is that reticence and coolness have either remained or else they have gradually brought to birth a more explicit approach. This should not surprise, given the veritable industry that the creation of new liturgies has become, and the sense of national identity fostered by the various provinces of the world-wide Anglican Communion.

The last ecumenical 'Statement' is the World Council of Churches Faith and Order Commission agreement on Baptism, Eucharist, and Ministry.[87] It reproduces the same kind of language as ARCIC, but with a stronger accent on the sacrifice of intercession, which is probably due to the influence of Max Thurian, of Taizé, who had written a remarkable study of the eucharist years before. 'Anamnesis' is 'both representation and anticipation', hence the essential movement of thanks and prayer as fundamental to the sacrificial character of the eucharist. 'In thanksgiving and intercession, the Church is united with the Son, its great High Priest and Intercessor (Rom 8.34, Heb 7.25).' The events of Christ's death and resurrection are not repeatable, yet 'the *anamnesis* of Christ is the basis and source of Christian prayer.' Furthermore, 'in Christ we offer ourselves as a living and holy sacrifice in our daily lives (Rom 12.1).' In these, and other ecumenical documents, it is a happy experience to see how the controversies of earlier centuries are gradually being healed, as well as how fresh perspectives are appearing on a story that will never be fully told this side of eternity.

XIII

Retrospect and Prospect

In an oft-quoted passage from his *Readings in St John's Gospel*, William Temple is inspired by Jesus' dialogue with the Samaritan woman (Jn 4.5–26) to reflect on the real purpose of worship:

> Both for perplexity and for dulled conscience the remedy is the same; sincere and spiritual worship. For worship is the submission of all our nature to God. It is the quickening of the conscience by His holiness; the nourishment of mind with His truth; the purifying of imagination by His beauty; the opening of the heart to His love; the surrender of will to His purpose – and all of this gathered up in adoration, the most selfless emotion of which our nature is capable and therefore the chief remedy for that self-centredness which is our original sin and the source of all actual sin.[88]

Such thoughts as these mix well with a discussion of eucharistic sacrifice, because they reflect on the tinge of pain which must run through the debate, for it has been not only an area of great diversity, but also at times of deep controversy between Christians. But if reflects, too, the profound joy of striking the gold that lies deep in the heart of sacrifice – self-giving and the nature of God himself. Are there any specific aspects to our story that require highlighting as we evaluate the kinds of movement in thought and practice in the past and see in them constructive pointers for the future?

First, it is worth observing that history is not cumulative, in the sense that ideas and insights simply pile up and provide a yet larger repertoire – or burden! – from which to draw out what is to be said in any given age. It is true that today we probably do possess more data about the eucharist (as indeed about many other things) than, for example, the Reformers. But the Church in its corporate life is not some kind of never-ending data-processing unit. It is, rather, an organism in which different elements are going to come together from different sources, in order to form what we may a times regard as a unity. Such a process is what structural anthropologists call *bricolage*, a term used to describe different kinds of human behaviour which vary according to circumstance but which by circumstance – as well as conscious decision – create patterns which in turn can institutionalise themselves into recognised norms if they gain enough strength and acceptance. We have watched how this happened in such a way as to form Anglican tradition, but it has been impossible to do so without viewing, too, the background from which it arose (mediaeval Catholicism), the other forces around at the Reformation (Protestantism), as well as the recovery sources that scholarship opened up (the early Fathers, and the East).

But the story is not always one of success. The Wesleyan revival proved too rich and different for the Church of England in the eighteenth century to absorb. (One wonders if things would have been different in the more open climate of our own time.) There are others who could be discussed, one of whom is Richard Baxter, whom we mentioned earlier, a Puritan who eventually left the Church of England at the Restoration even though he was offered a bishopric. He had a strong doctrine of eucharistic sacrifice which had much in common with Taylor's heavenly priesthood of Christ, but which was enriched by covenant theology and had a dynamic view of the 'actualisation' of the eucharistic celebration, in bread broken and wine out-poured.[89]

Nor is the story always one of ever-expanding development. We noted Max Thurian's strong accent on the eucharist as sacrifice of praise and supplication, an insight gained from careful reflection on the Jewish roots of the eucharistic prayer. But he did not get there first! When Alexander Jolly over a century earlier was explaining our theme to his readers, he took care to adopt exactly the same approach:

> Thus, we enforce every prayer *Through Jesus Christ*, but still more hopefully and prevalently when we offer them in the eucharist, which is the sacrifice of prayer, as well as of praise and thanksgiving.[90]

Secondly, we noted how Will Spens began his discussion of sacrifice from the point of view of social anthropology. A few words need to be said about this. While this kind of approach is by no means a single, united school of thought, it has certain rules of thumb which can throw light on the eucharist. It distinguishes between feeding and eating – feeding being a deliberate, conscious action by the community in performing a ritual by which it can reduce the deity to manageable chunks, and do so in solidarity with others, as an expression of corporate resolve and faith. The ritual form has to be handed down in patterned and accepted words and actions – and that includes music. Such a ritual meal is described as 'commensual'. But there is another kind of ritual meal which is intended to deal with pollution, the community's and the individual's sin. Such a meal is termed 'piacular', and it is subject to the same kind of forces, repetition, familiarity, identity – and a sense of handing on something important for generations to come.[91] At this most basic level, liturgy and doctrine, worship and the understanding it embodies and feeds, have to live in a reciprocal relationship if they are to survive intact. In this fascinating process, the eucharist has a certain autonomy, never quite becoming the servant either of the liturgist or the theologian.

There is no doubt that both these insights have a direct bearing on the eucharist, both in terms of solidarity and feeding, and in the desire to handle sin as a regular feature of human existence. In that respect, the eucharist is viewed comparatively with other religious activities. But matters cannot simply be left there, because the question has to be asked, in what sense is the eucharist unique among all these religious meals? The obvious answer is to say that Jesus Christ is the unique revelation of the eternal deity, God Himself, a revelation made known to us and celebrated among us in the power of the Holy Spirit. On this showing, the eucharist is the fulfilment of every meal, religious included, for it is celebrated as a sign that God uses ritual patterns and forms in order to enter into and transform *all* human culture. As Paul Avis has remarked, 'Christian identity is dependent on cultural norms. It settles into the shape determined by the available ideological receptacles.'[92]

Thirdly, such social anthropological observations carry their own caution against arguing too much and too precisely, and too little and too vaguely, for what the eucharist is there to do. We have seen how the Reformers reacted against a pastoral practice, and a theology undergirding it, which made the eucharist become 'offered for' certain very specific requests, so that this aspect becomes too dominant and forces other necessary ones, e.g. thanksgiving, out of the scene. Similarly, to use the language of 'propitiation' of the eucharist, as in some sense appeasing an angry deity, is to give it an independent life for which it was not originally designed. The lesson of the tale is to affirm that, as with presence, and much else, all language, all principal theological expressions, are by their nature *derivative* and *secondary*, derivative of and secondary to Christ's presence and Christ's sacrifice.

The eucharist is bound to draw to itself the imagery and language of how people interpret Christ's death, the most enduring being those which speak of God *absorbing* sin and death through his eternal act of love in Christ.[93] On the other hand, Reformation sensitivity about sacrifice must not result in handling every piece of imagery as if with a long pair of conceptual tongs, otherwise all creative writing and artistic aspiration would be stunted at birth. Furthermore, a traditional Anglican 'coolness' and 'reticence' about sacrifice could disappear into a haze of vagueness, in which the eucharist might be this, or might be that, and you can pick and choose what you like. That would be to reduce the eucharist to something far less than it properly is, and devalue it in the faith and practice of the community. In some lectures delivered in his sage-like retirement, Michael Ramsey, former Archbishop of Canterbury (1904–1988), went with customary acuity to the nub of the matter:

> It will be apparent how close is Christ's sacrifice to the Eucharist, for there his sacrifice is present both in that aspect which is solitary and unshared and in that aspect in which the faithful participate.[94]

In other words, Calvary and Supper are connected but distinct, and – in quite different ways – very real.

Fourthly, when it comes to liturgical presentation, we immediately enter a scene in which doctrine is reflected in action. There are three main different ways in which the Anglican eucharist has been, and continues to be, celebrated, and each has its own emphasis. The old format of the priest at the north end of the altar, and an assistant at the south end, is that to which our seventeenth century divines were accustomed. The priest standing in the centre, facing east, is probably the most deeply traditional in Christianity, and it was gradually recovered in many places in the nineteenth century. Finally, to celebrate the eucharist around the table, manifestly popular in our own day, but not quite as 'primitive' as the enthusiasts argue, has added a third style to the tradition.[95]

Without providing too schematic an analysis of this diverse picture, we can offer a mildly theological rationale. The 'north-south-end' style reflects the fact that *Jesus* is the celebrant, joining the eucharist with his prayers in heaven. The eastward position expresses the offering of a memorial sacrifice, as the whole congregation faces the same way, making that memorial until he comes again. Celebration facing the congregation has the effect of gathering the community around the holy table and can only serve to heighten the sense of fellowship, solidarity, unity, and covenant-renewal which is part of much contemporary Christianity. Inevitably, choices have to be made, for it would be impossible to use all three at the same celebration! On the other hand, the historian has the twofold task of explaining how and why we have got where we have, and to suggest – particularly in an Anglican context – that no one method in fact manages to express everything. When Gregory Dix published his masterpiece, *The Shape of the Liturgy*, he provided a much-needed stimulus for many people to see the history of the eucharist in a fresh light. But his popularisation of the 'offertory procession' not only lacked firm foundations in antiquity, it needed a pastoral corrective.[96] And when many years ago Michael Ramsey criticised it as 'a shallow and romantic sort of Pelagianism', he was reminding us all that however eloquent the action of people bringing forward the bread and wine for the eucharistic celebration, we come at the end of the day with nothing but what God has provided already.[97]

Fifthly, it would be tempting as we draw near to the end of an exploration of the story of the Anglican eucharist to give the impression that presence and sacrifice – in isolation from each other and everything else – are what it is all about. In a book-review some years ago, Leslie Houlden gave a gentle warning that incarnation and atonement ran the risk of looming so large on the christological landscape that they can stand out too sharply. 'Once peaks in a landscape full of hills, all seen as such instances, they now stand out like naked pillars of rock in a plain.'[98] Although our study has focused on the twin-themes of presence and sacrifice, we have set out to show that it is impossible to reflect seriously on the eucharist without seeing presence and sacrifice in relation to each other, and also spilling out – like hills on a plain – onto other key-motifs, such as penitence, reneweal, the Spirit, the Trinity, and, above all, the work of Christ.

One of the ways in which such a unifying of concepts develops and comes across in celebration is through the power of 'iteration' – the formal repetition of ritual words and actions. But the words that appear in liturgies, and the language used by theological commentators, still matter a great deal. To borrow an image from the stage, a weak libretto has a limited life, regardless of the quality of the actors or the stage-set. And that is why Anglicans perhaps need to be more conscious of the inner advantages of possessing a fine literary culture, which continues to sustain the worshipping and reflective life of the community. If there is one crucial insight from the Anglican story, it is the need to see sacrifice in a wide, not a narrow context. It is simply too rich, too near the heart of Christianity, to survive over-definition, on the one hand, or woolly sentimentality, on the other. To put it bluntly, the eucharist keeps coming back for more, for we shall never fully understand its deep, rich, and mysterious character.

XIV

Anglican Identity?

Is there something specifically Anglican in what we have said so far? More is at stake than just a doctrine – or doctrines – of eucharistic sacrifice. Indeed, one of the limitations of any survey of such a tantalising subject is the criteria of selection. The authors so far have all been from the British Isles, with one exception they have been male, and nearly of them have been ordained. That is clearly not going to be the case in the future. Much more important, we have not dealt with the more general issue of inculturation, which is bound to become increasingly important as the eucharist enters cultures in which sacrifice has been – or continues to be – very much part of the surrounding religious and conceptual scene. The Korean liturgy has some interesting insights here over the language of offering, precisely because of the need to translate the liturgy into words that will have dignity and reality.[99] It is our conviction that the story will repeat itself, as the eucharist adapts into new environments because it will always have the inner resources – God given – to do so.

But what of that Anglican identity? Many of the things we have said are found in close parallel among theologians of the Reformed tradition like Alasdair Heron, Roman Catholics such as David Power, and Methodists of the stature of Geoffrey Wainwright.[100] Each one of them has made a considerable impact on the eucharistic life of the Christian community beyond the confines of their own churches, Heron alerting his tradition to some of its weaknesses, Power proclaiming the dynamism of narrative within the eucharistic assembly's self-identity, and Wainwright providing a synthesis of worship and life that draws on the best of tradition while still challenging separated Christians today to live up to their calling. It may well be true that the word 'plead' made one of its first appearances in Simon Patrick's *Mensa Mystica* in 1660. But it only appears in a *liturgy* in the Reformed tradition in our own century, though it has been proposed for an alternative eucharistic prayer in the Church of England.[101] The future may well hold a much more varied story over what it is to be Anglican in eucharistic theology as a whole, but in any case, to hold to an identity at all is about being secure, not looking for points of division. Anglicans need both to know and to love their own tradition. They need to do so in order to be secure within it; to see its perspectives, potentials and limitations; and to be able to articulate it in a world that is full of surprises, which will include people from other Churches wanting to know more about it themselves.[102]

But life continues to be lived in paradoxes. The present writer spent some months in 1983 teaching in a Roman Catholic University in the Mid-West of the USA, in the course of which he had to give some lectures on the history of the eucharist. One of the real points of difficulty was to describe the kind of late medieval eucharistic piety that produced such a counter-reaction at the Reformation. Every visual aid was tried in the lecture, some taped music, liturgical texts – not to score points, simply to describe and explain. At the end of the session, an undergraduate, who was not trying to be polite to a visiting Anglican, stated quietly but firmly: 'we don't understand this – the mass for us is first and foremost a *celebration*'. The mind went back to Thomas Aquinas, who in a set of prayers written by him for the feast of Corpus Christi taught that the eucharist was a memorial of the passion, the food of the Church, and a prefiguring for future glory – a threefold scheme not dissimilar from the memorial, covenant, and heavenly offering we have suggested as foundational elements in our quest.[103]

Yet, one cannot but regret that in one of the new eucharistic prayers (no. IV) written in the wake of the liturgical reforms after the Second Vatican Council, the words 'we offer you his body and blood' appear for the first time in a eucharistic prayer even though such a formulation had been accepted by some Catholic theologians for centuries.[104] What goes into a prayer matters a great deal, and an age of ecumenical rapprochement of necessity engenders a certain degree of wider scrutiny. On the other hand, one can still make a virtue from over-reacting against 'offering Christ's body' to God in the eucharist, not least where 'celebration' has become the dominant motif, to the exclusion of all else. To miss out on the awe and the cost of the metaphor of sacrifice is to diminish the total dynamism of the Lord's Supper. Anglicanism at its best tries to grapple with precisely this rich ambiguity in a constructive manner.

For all the remaining (and diminishing) points of controversy at the ecumenical level, and the liturgical diversity in the worldwide Anglican Communion, it still remains possible to say that there are significant criteria for suggesting an Anglican approach to the question.[105] In a recent essay on Anglican eucharistic theology, Christopher Cocksworth has drawn attention to what he calls 'unitive categories' in eucharistic theology as a whole.[106] When he comes to sacrifice, he highlights three. The first is 'proclamation', a biblical model that provides the eucharist with the sense of *doing* something before God – shades of Andrewes' caution against mere mental activity. The second is 'sacrifice of praise', another biblical term which evokes the sense of *celebrating* the Lord's death – shades of Patrick's language of delight. The third is 'union with Christ', more problematic because of how it finds expression, but nonetheless profoundly Christian – shades of Parsons' hymn that mentions 'pleading thy perfect work of love.'

There are two further factors that have lurked in the background of much of our discussion. One is the relationship between the liturgical text of the Church and the way it is interpreted, and celebrated. We noted the Prayer Book rite, and the pressures from the eighteenth century down to our own time to adapt it, or to compose afresh within its ethos and style. We have observed, too, the ways in which sacrifice has been *reinterpreted* in new generations. It really is a remarkably adhesive aroma! The other is the way in which the eucharistic sacrifice at its most authentic enters into the life of the Trinity. Our discussion of the 'heavenly offering' showed how vital it is to have an understanding of God that points continually to the future, as the Church prays not only for the blessing of the gifts and the communicants, but that the whole celebration may continue to transform the environment in which it takes place. For at the end of the day, any perspective of the Lord's Supper which is specifically sacrificial must be about the work of the Trinity, for it is ultimately God's triumph in human hearts and lives, as they offer their sacrifice of memory, covenant and prayer in the power of the Spirit, through the Son's eternal self-oblation, to the Father of lights in heaven.[107]

One suspects that future paths may well place increasing emphasis on notions of time and eternity, and the work of the Spirit as transforming power, as Andrewes kept saying in his sermons. Moreover, it is to be hoped that ways of reaching lay eucharistic piety can be found and expressed along these lines, particularly when one bears in mind that classical writers like Taylor, Patrick, Brevint and Bickersteth illustrated their writings with devotional prayers for the lay audience they were stimulating and nurturing. There is a danger that prayer-writers will produce fine new liturgies, replete with excellent sources and fine cadences, and then leave the worshipper in the lurch with no devotional nourishment by which to make the vital connection between 'my life as I live it the rest of the week' and the total, sometimes aggressively corporate Sunday eucharistic celebration. New paths followed with zeal and imagination have a habit of producing new opportunities, new tasks.

Henry Chadwick once remarked, in referring to Augustine's discussion of memory (*Confessions* X), that 'the memory of the past is decisive for interpreting the present.'[108] One of the motivations for this discussion is to bring out of that rich cavern which makes up our common memory treasures that can not only tell us how we have got where we are, but also point to where we might go in the years to come. As Thomas Traherne remarks in his *Centuries of Meditations*:

> Men do mightily wrong themselves when they refuse to be present in all ages.

And he goes on:

> By seeing the Saints of all Ages we are present with them.[109]

Meanwhile, what Anglicans have in common is a conviction that the liturgy and the faith of the Church live side by side, and that both are to be trusted to embody a living tradition, where riches are conserved, and we are not afraid of paradox or ambiguity, not least when we gather around that table. It is only part of the story, a story worth knowing and loving not only for its own sake but in the face of the opportunities that lie ahead. But it is, too, a precious and costly narrative that points to a forgiving and gracious God, whose nature is nothing more and nothing less than self-giving love.

NOTES TO PART TWO

1. *Didache* 14.2; see R.C.D. Jasper, G.J. Cuming (eds.) *The Prayers of the Eucharist: Early and Reformed* (New York: Pueblo, 1987), p. 24: 'But let none who has a quarrel with his companion join with you until they have been reconciled, that your sacrifice may not be defiled.'
2. Hippolytus, *Apostolic Tradition* 4.12; see Jasper/Cuming, *op.cit.*, p.35: 'remembering therefore his death and resurrection, we offer to you the bread and the cup, giving thanks because you have held us worthy to stand before you and minister to you.' The sacrificial imagery of the final clause is consistently underplayed or ignored by those who comment on this much-discussed prayer.

3. See Kenneth Stevenson, *Eucharist and Offering* (with foreword by Mark Santer), (New York: Pueblo, 1986).
4. See Thomas J. Talley, 'The Windsor Statement and the Eucharistic Prayer', in Thomas J. Talley, *Worship: Reforming Tradition* (Washington: Pastoral Press, 1990) pp. 38f.; for whole essay, pp. 35–46, in which Talley discusses modern eucharistic prayers, including Roman Catholic, in relation to the ARCIC 'Statement'.
5. See, for example, David N. Power, *The Sacrifice We Offer: The Tridentine Dogma and Its Reinterpretation* (Edinburgh: T and T Clark, 1987). Power suggests that the real issue at Trent for Protestants is not the eucharistic sacrifice so much as the office of the priest.
6. See *Archbishop Cranmer on The Sacrament of the Lord's Supper* (Parker Society) (Cambridge: University Press, 1854) pp. 345ff.
7. See The *Workes of that Famous and Worthy Minister of Christ in the University of Cambridge, M. William Perkins* (Volume II) (Cambridge: Legatt, 1613), p. 552. See also, in general, Bryan D. Spinks, *From the Lord and 'The Best Reformed Churches': A study of the eucharistic liturgy in the English Puritan and Separatist traditions 1550–1633* (Bibliotheca Ephemerides Liturgicae 'Subsidia' 33) (Roma: Edizioni Liturgiche, 1984).
8. See *Anglican Orders (English): The Bull of His Holiness Leo XIII, Sept. 13th, 1896, and the Answer of the Archbishops of England, March 29th, 1897* (Church Historical Society) (London: S.P.C.K., 1932), XI.17 (p. 35).
9. See the various works of Colin Buchanan, *Modern Anglican Liturgies (1958–1968)* (London: Oxford University Press, 1968); *Further Anglican Liturgies 1968–1975* (Bramcote: Grove Books, 1975); and *Latest Anglican Liturgies (1976-1984)* (London: S.P.C.K./ Grove Books, 1985).
10. See Frances M. Young, *Sacrifice and the Death of Christ* (London: S.P.C.K., 1975).
11. J.L. Houlden, 'Sacrifice and the Eucharist', in Ian Ramsey (ed.), *Thinking about the Eucharist: Papers by members of the Church of England Doctrine Commission* (London: S.C.M., 1972) pp. 95f.; for whole essay, see pp. 81–98.
12. Quoted from *Poetry and Prose of John Donne* (selected and edited by A. Desmond Hawkins) (London: Nelson, 1938), p. 357; also in P.E. More, F.L. Cross (eds.) *Anglicanism: The Thought and Practice of the Church of England, Illustrated from the Religious Literature of the Seventeenth Century* (London: S.P.C.K., 1951) no. 357 (p. 774).
13. Quoted from *The Poems of George Herbert* (with an Introduction by Arthur Waugh) (London: Oxford University Press, 1907), p. 163; also in Darwell Stone, *A History of the Doctrine of the Holy Eucharist* (Vol. II) (London: Longmans, 1909) (hereafter referred to as *Darwell Stone II*) pp. 278f.

14. See *Centuries of Meditations by Thomas Traherne* (edited by Bertram Doble) (London: Doble, 1908) pp. 70f (Century I.92); and A.M. Allchin, Anne Ridler, Julia Smith, *Profitable Wonders: Aspects of Thomas Traherne* (Oxford: Amate Press, 1989), p. 52 (Select Meditiations II, 77); see also *ibid.*, for a discussion of Traherne's life, and his various works.

15. See Rowan Williams, *After Silent Centuries* (Oxford: Perpetua Press, 1994), p. 33.

16. See Kenneth Stevenson, 'Eucharistic Sacrifice: An Insoluble Liturgical Problem?', in *Scottish Journal of Theology* 42 (1989) pp. 469–492 (reprinted in Kenneth W. Stevenson, *Worship: Wonderful and Sacred Mystery* (Washington: Pastoral Press, 1992) pp. 43–68.)

17. Jeremy Taylor, *The Worthy Communicant* (London: Norton, 1660), see frontispiece.

18. See Bryan D. Spinks, *The sanctus in the eucharistic prayer* (Cambridge: University Press, 1991).

19. *Saint Augustine: Confessions* (translated with an introduction and notes by Henry Chadwick) (Oxford: Clarendon Press, 1991) xxi (27) (p. 236).

20. *ibid.* xi (18) p. 189.

21. English translation in *Darwell Stone* II, p. 265.

22. see above n.8.

23. *Darwell Stone* II, p. 266.

24. For a discussion of this, see Kenneth Stevenson, *Covenant of Grace Renewed: A Vision of the Eucharist in the Seventeenth Century* (London: Darton, Longman and Todd, 1994) pp. 46–53.

25. Quoted from *ibid.* p. 58 (translation by David Scott).

26. See *The Works of William Laud* II (Library of Anglo-Catholic Theology) (Oxford: Parker, 1853) pp. 328ff and 339ff.

27. See *Considerationes Modestae et Pacificae* (Library of Anglo-Catholic Theology) (Oxford: Parker, 1846) pp. 576–579.

28. *ibid.* pp. 612–613. Cf. J.B. Mozley's distinction between 'original' and 'derivative' propitiation, which serves to retain the powerful and passionate language of propitiation (in relation to the cross) and gives the eucharist a place within that movement; see *Darwell Stone* II pp. 579f; also see J. B. Mozley *Lectures and Other Theological Papers* (London: Rivington, 1883), p. 217.

29. Daniel Waterland, *A Review of the Doctrine of the Holy Eucharist* (Oxford: Clarendon, 1896) pp. 344f. I am grateful to the Bishop of Newcastle, Alec Graham, for a copy of 'Daniel Waterland and the Eucharist', a sermon preached by him before the University of Cambridge, Sunday 13th October 1991.

30. See above n. 3.

31. A comparable approach is adopted by Herbert Thorndike (see *Covenant of Grace Renewed* pp. 144ff.) whom we shall be looking at later.

32. (Thomas Rattray), *Some Particular Instructions Concerning the Christian Covenant and the Mysteries by which it is Transacted and Maintained* (London: Bettenham, 1748) pp. 23–25. See also *Darwell Stone* II p. 617. See also A.M. Allchin, 'Thomas Rattray: after 250 years', a lecture delivered in St Mary's Cathedral, Edinburgh, 22nd May, 1994, in conjunction with a celebration of Rattray's liturgy.
33. F. Meyrick, *The Doctrine of the Church of England on the Holy Communion* (London: Longmans, 1908) pp. 201f.
34. *ibid.* p. 203.
35. see *Darwell Stone* II p. 556.
36. see Maurice Frost (ed), *Historical Companion to Hymns Ancient and Modern* (London: Clowes, 1962) pp. 349f.
37. Gregory Dix, *The Treatise on The Apostolic Tradition of St Hippolytus of Rome* (Church Historical Society) (London: S.P.C.K., 1937) p. 73.
38. see below n. 100.
39. see above n. 16.
40. A recent study is John Dunnill, *Covenant and Sacrifice in The Letter to the Hebrews* (Cambridge: University Press, 1993).
41. Richard Hooker, *Laws of Ecclesiastical Polity* V; quotations from 56.11; 60.2; 57.5; 67.7; 67.13. See also *Covenant of Grace Renewed* pp. 25ff.
42. Ralph Cudworth, *A Discourse Concerning the True Notion of the Lord's Supper* (London: Cotes, 1642); reprinted in Thomas Birch (ed), *The Works of Ralph Cudworth* (Volume IV) (Oxford: University Press, 1829).
43. See *Covenant of Grace Renewed, passim.* See also Peter Toon, *Justification and Sanctification* (London: Marshall, Morgan and Scott, 1983).
44. See Cudworth, *A Discourse*, pp. 69f.; and Birch (ed), *The Works of Ralph Cudworth* (Volume IV) pp. 276ff.
45. See *The Theological Works of Herbert Thorndike* (Library of Anglo-Catholic Theology) (Oxford: Parker, 1844), Volume IV, Part 1, pp. 103, 17f., 102, 118. In an unpubished discourse he refers to the self-offering as 'nothing else, but the formal and express reprising of the Covenant of Baptism on our part.' (Wesminster Abbey Library, Th MS 2/1/4 p.1.) See in general *Covenant of Grace Renewed* pp. 143ff.
46. See Simon Patrick, *Mensa Mystica: or, A Discourse Concerning the Sacrament of the Lord's Supper* (London: Tyton 1684) pp. 4, 13, 36f., 51, 58; and Alexander Taylor (ed), *The Works of Simon Patrick, including his Autobiography* (Oxford: University Press, 1858) Vol. I, pp. 94f, 114f., 119, 122f., 126. See also *Covenant of Grace Renewed* pp. 151ff. See also Kenneth Stevenson, 'The eucharistic theology of Simon Patrick', in Carsten Bach-Nielsen,

Susanne Gregersen, Ninna Jørgensen, *Ordet, Kirken, og Kulturen: Afhandlinger om Kristendomshistorie tilegnet til Jakob Balling* (Aarhus: Universitetsforlag, 1993) pp. 363–378.

47. F.D. Maurice, *The Kingdom of Christ: Or Hints to a Quaker, respecting the Principles, Constitution, and Ordinances of the Catholic Church* (Volume II) (London: Rivington, 1842) (2nd edition) pp. 92f.

48. William Temple, *Christus Veritas: An Essay* (London: Macmillan, 1925) pp. 163, 238f., 241f.

49. Rowan Williams, *Eucharistic Sacrifice – The Roots of a Metaphor* (Grove Liturgical Study 31) (Bramcote: Grove, 1982), p. 27.

50. Rowan Williams, *Resurrection: Interpreting the Easter Gospel* (London: Darton, Longman, and Todd, 1982) pp. 111f.

51. See D.H. Tripp, *The Renewal of the Covenant in the Methodist Tradition* (London: Epworth, 1969).

52. See the discussion of this questions, among others, in Rowan Williams, 'Imagining the Kingdom: Questions for Anglican Worship Today', in Kenneth Stevenson, Bryan Spinks (eds), *The Identity of Anglican Worship* (London: Mowbrays, 1991) pp. 1–13.

53. *The Book of Common Prayer* (New York: Church Hymnal Corporation, 1979) p. 365.

54. See, for example, Peter Forster, 'Some Reflections on the Theology of Thomas Cranmer', in Margot Johnson (ed), *Thomas Cranmer: Essays in Commemoration of the 500th Anniversary of his Birth* (Durham: Turnstone Ventures, 1990) pp. 253–271.

55. See in particular, Christopher J. Cocksworth, *Evangelical Eucharistic Thought in the Church of England* (Cambridge: University Press, 1993) esp. pp. 24ff; and Bryan D. Spinks, 'The Ascension and the Vicarious Humanity of Christ: The Christology and Soteriology Behind the Church of Scotland's Anamnesis and Epiklesis', in J. Neil Alexander (ed), *Time and Community: in Honor of Thomas Julian Talley* (Washington: Pastoral Press, 1990), pp. 185–201.

56. See Taylor, *The Worthy Communicant* (cited above n.17) p. 74ff; and *The Whole Works of Jeremy Taylor* (edited by Reginald Heber, revised and corrected by Charles Eden) (Volume VIII) (London: Longmans, 1852) pp. 37f. See also the classic treatment, H.R. McAdoo, *The Eucharistic Theology of Jeremy Taylor Today* (Norwich: Canterbury Press, 1988); and *Covenant of Grace Renewed*, pp. 115ff.

57. *Worthy Communicant*, pp. 79f; and *The Whole Works of Jeremy Taylor* (Volume VIII) p. 40.

58. See Daniel Brevint, *The Christian Sacrament and Sacrifice: By way of Discourse, Meditation, and Prayer* (Oxford: Vincent, 1847) pp. 37f (Section IV.11), and pp. 66f (Section VII.9); see also *Covenant of Grace Renewed*, pp. 99ff.

59. See Henry McAdoo, 'A Theology of the Eucharist: Brevint and the Wesleys', *Theology* July/August 1994, xcvii, No. 778, pp. 245–256.

60. Edward Bickersteth, *A Treatise on the Lord's Supper* (London: L.B. Seeley and Son, 1824) p. 61. As Cocksworth, who quotes him, notes, he does not give his source for the quotation; see *Evangelical Eucharistic Thought in the Church of England*, p. 75 and p. 240 n.84.

61. Nathaniel Dimock, *The Doctrine of the Lord's Supper* (London: Longmans, 1910), p. 51; quoted in Cocksworth, *Evangelical Eucharistic Thought in the Church of England* p. 83. See also (N. Dimock), *On Eucharistic Worship in the English Church* (London: Haughton, 1876) p. 232. 'In this sacrifice all is not what it is, not in real being, nor by any real objective presence, but in the way of vicarious representation, and ordained commemoration ... Christians had in the highest sense ... no real sacrifice to offer, because their one all-sufficient Sacrifice of propitiation had already, and once for all, been offered and accepted. They had learned to come before God as, in themselves, beggars, with nothing to give and all to receive.'

62. Alexander Jolly, *The Christian Sacrifice in the Eucharist; considered as it is the Doctrine of Holy Scripture, embraced by the Universal Church of the First and Purest Times, by the Church of England and by the Episcopal Church in Scotland* (Aberdeen: Brown, 1831) pp. 191f. (Quoted, in part, in Meyrick, *The Doctrine of the Church of England on the Holy Communion*, pp. 67f.) The heavenly intercession of Christ, pleaded by the Church, is a recurring motif throughout this work.

63. R.I. Wilberforce, *The Doctrine of the Holy Eucharist* (London: Mozley, 1853) pp. 351, 352.

64. Quoted from Alf Härdelin, *The Tractarian Understanding of the Eucharist* (Acta Univesitatis Upaliensis: Studia Historico-Ecclesiastica Upsaliensia 8) (Uppsala: Almqvist and Wiksells, 1965), p. 216 (Wilberforce) and p. 205 n.40 (Pusey).

65. See *Covenant of Grace Renewed* pp. 162f. n.40. For McAdoo on Taylor, see *The Eucharistic Theology of Jeremy Taylor Today* pp. 65f. Francis Paget, one of the original drafters of the Archbishops' reply to Pope Leo XIII's bull (see above n.8) uses the term 'pleading of the sacrifice' more than once in correspondence, which makes one assume it to have been a commonplace; see Stephen Paget and J.M.C. Crum, *Francis Paget* (London: Macmillan, 1912) pp. 107f. On the use of the term in Reformed liturgies, see J.M. Barkley, '"Pleading His Eternal Sacrifice" in the Reformed Liturgy', in Bryan D. Spinks (ed), *The Sacrifice of Praise: Studies on the themes of thanksgiving and redemption in the central prayers of the eucharistic and baptismal liturgies* (Bibliotheca

Ephemerides Liturgicae 'Subsidia' 19) (Rome: Edizioni Liturgiche, 1981), pp. 123–140.

66. Richard Godfrey Parsons, *The Sacrament of Sacrifice* (London: Longmans, 1936) pp. 27f.

67. *ibid* p. 62.

68. Augustine, *De Civitate Dei* 10.xx; see *The City of God (de Civitate Dei)* (a translation into English) (Volume I) (The Ancient and Modern Library of Theological Literature) (London: Griffith Farran Okeden and Welsh, n.d.) p. 297.

69. See, for a detailed discussion, with references, Kenneth Stevenson, ' "The unbloody sacrifice": The Origins and development of a description of the Eucharist', in Gerard Austin (ed), *Fountain of Life: In Memory of Niels K. Rasmussen, O.P.* (Washington: Pastoral Press, 1991) pp. 103–130. The original text is Testament of Levi 3.3–5.

70. See *Darwell Stone II* p. 230.

71. Charles Gore, *The Body of Christ: An Enquiry into the Institution and Doctrine of Holy Communion* (London: Murray, 1901) pp. 161f.

72. See works cited above n.9; for an Evangelical perspective, see Colin Buchanan, *The End of the Offertory – An Anglican Study* (Grove Liturgical Study 14) (Bramcote: Grove, 1978).

73. See *The Book of Alternative Services of the Anglican Church of Canada* (Toronto: Anglican Book Centre, 1985).

74. See Williams, *Easter* p. 111.

75. See *Ninety-Six Sermons by Lancelot Andrewes* (Library of Anglo-Catholic Theology) (Oxford: Parker, 1841). The references in each of the sermons as cited are as follows: Volume V pp. 67f; I, p. 84; II p. 402; V p. 94; I p. 194; I p. 214; III p. 161; I p.247; II p. 250; and II pp. 299ff. See also Nicholas Lossky, *Lancelot Andrewes The Preacher (1555–1626): The Origins of the Mystical Theology of the Church of England* (Oxford: Clarendon Press, 1991). On memory, see Malcolm Guite, 'The Art of Memory and the Art of Salvation', Durham PhD thesis, 1993, pp. 109–174, on Andrewes. It is to be hoped that this original study will be published one day.

76. See J. Ernest Rattenbury, *The Eucharistic Hymns of John and Charles Wesley* (London: Epworth, 1948). This consists of a study of the hymns, and their background, together with a reprint of the abridgement of Brevint. The hymns are printed in full at the end. Those quoted here are: no. 3 (p. 196); no. 129 (p. 236); and no. 157 (p. 245). See also Cocksworth, *Evangelical Eucharistic Thought in the Church of England*, pp. 63ff., and McAdoo article, above n.59.

77. See above n.58.

78. See Will Spens, 'The Eucharist', in E.G. Selwyn (ed), *Essays Catholic and Critical* (London: S.P.C.K., 1926) pp. 430, and 438f.

79. See Evelyn Underhill, *Worship* (London: Nisbet, 1936) p. 147.
80. Evelyn Underhill, *The Mystery of Sacrifice* (London: Longmans, 1938) p. 15.
81. *Worship*, pp. 234f.
82. See Todd E. Johnson, 'Pneumatological Oblation: Evelyn Underhill's Theology of the Eucharist', *Worship* 68.4 (1994) pp. 313--332.
83. C.O. Buchanan, E.L. Mascall, J.I. Packer, The Bishop of Willesden, *Growing into Union: Proposals for forming a united Church in England* (London: S.P.C.K., 1970) p. 191.
84. Anglican-Roman Catholic International Commission, *The Final Report* (Windsor, 1981) (London: C.T.S./S.P.C.K., 1981) III, The Eucharist and the Sacrifice of Christ, 5 (pp. 13f.)
85. See Buchanan, *Latest Anglican Liturgies* p. 88.
86. *ibid* p. 58.
87. *Baptism, Eucharist, and Ministry* (Faith and Order Paper No. 111) (Geneva: World Council of Churches, 1982) II The Meaning of the Eucharist, B The Eucharist as Anamnesis or Memorial of Christ (pp. 11f.). See also Max Thurian, *L'Eucharistie: Mémorial du Seigneur, Sacrifice d'Action de Grâce et d'Intercession* (Neuchatel/ Paris: Delachaux et Niestlé, 1959); translated into English as *The Eucharistic Memorial* (Ecumenical Studies in Worship 7 and 8) (London: Lutterworth, 1960, 1961).
88. William Temple, *Readings in St John's Gospel* (London: Macmillan, 1952) p. 68.
89. On Baxter, see Stevenson, *Covenant of Grace Renewed*, pp. 126ff. See, in particular, Bryan D. Spinks 'Two Seventeenth-Century Examples of *Lex Credendi, Lex Orandi*: The Baptismal and Eucharistic Liturgies of Jeremy Taylor and Richard Baxter', *Studia Liturgica* 21 (1991) pp. 165–189.
90. See Jolly, *The Christian Sacrifice* p. 73.
91. See Stevenson, *Eucharist and Offering* pp. 228ff. See also Mary Douglas, *Purity and Danger* (London: Routledge and Kegan Paul, 1966); and also Christopher Walsh, 'Liturgy and Symbolism: A Map' in Kenneth Stevenson (ed.), *Symbolism and the Liturgy* (Grove Liturgical Study 23) (Bramcote: Grove Books, 1980) pp. 17–26.
92. Paul Avis, *Anglicanism and the Christian Church* (Edinburgh: T and T Clark, 1989) p. 302.
93. See, for example, F.W. Dillistone, *The Christian Understanding of Atonement* (2nd edition) (London: S.C.M., 1984), esp. pp. 29ff, 216ff.
94. Michael Ramsey, *Jesus and the Living Past* (Oxford: University Press, 1980) p. 74.
95. See Jaime Lara, '*Versus Populum* Revisited', *Worship* 68 (1994) pp. 210–221.

96. Gregory Dix, *The Shape of the Liturgy* (London: Dacre/A.C. Black, 1945). For an evaluation of his work, see Kenneth Stevenson, *Gregory Dix – 25 Years On* (Grove Liturgical Study 10) (Bramcote: Grove, 1977) p. 23f.
97. A.M. Ramsey, *Durham Essays and Addresses* (London: S.P.C.K. 1956), p. 18.
98. Leslie Houlden, Review of W.J. Abraham, *Divine Revelation and the Limits of Historical Criticism*, in *Journal of Theological Studies* 34.1 (April 1983) p. 378; quoted by Maurice Wiles at the start of his essay, 'A Naked Pillar of Rock', in Stephen Barton and Graham Stanton (eds.), *Resurrection: Essays in Honour of Leslie Houlden* (London: S.P.C.K., 1994) p. 116. I am indebted to my colleague, Stephen Baker, for insights in this discussion.
99. See Buchanan, *Further Anglican Liturgies* pp. 298ff. See also David R. Holeton, *Liturgical Inculturation in the Anglican Communion* (Alcuin/GROW Liturgical Study 15) (Bramcote: Grove, 1990); and also Phillip Tovey, *Inculturation: The Eucharist in Africa* (Alcuin/GROW Liturgical Study 7) (Bramcote: Grove, 1988).
100. See Alasdair Heron, *Table and Tradition: Towards an Ecumenical Understanding of the Eucharist* (Edinburgh: Handsel Press, 1983) pp. 167ff on the relationship between Christ's offering and ours; (see also T.F. Torrance, 'The Mind of Christ in Worship: The Problem of Apollinarianism in the Liturgy', in *Theology in Reconciliation* (London: Chapman, 1975) pp. 132ff., on the self-offering of Christ;) David N. Power, *The Eucharistic Mystery: Revitalizing the Tradition* (New York: Crossroad, 1992) pp. 320ff., almost prophetic on the language of metaphor in sacrifice; and Geoffrey Wainwright, *Doxology: The Praise of God in Worship, Doctrine and Life – A Systematic Theology* (London: Epworth, 1980) pp. 271ff on 'anamnesis' and pleading the sacrifice.
101. See Spinks article, n.55 above; it first appeared in the 1932 rite of the United Church of Canada, and thereafter was used in the 1940 Scottish Book of Common Order. For the Church of England eucharistic prayer, see *Patterns for Worship: A Report by the Liturgical Commission of the General Synod of the Church of England* (London: Church House Publishing, 1989) p. 244. Power also uses the word 'plead' of the eucharistic action, *The Eucharistic Mystery*, p. 185.
102. For direct evidence of this, see above, n.75, for the seminal study of Andrewes' preaching, written originally in French by Nicholas Lossky, a Russian Orthodox lay theologian; and one of the most significant studies on Richard Hooker is by Olivier Loyer, a French Roman Catholic, who died before there was ever a thought that it too might be translated into English, see Olivier Loyer, *L'anglicanisme de Richard Hooker* (2 Volumes) (thèse présentée devant l'université de Paris III – le 1 juin, 1977) (Paris: Librairie Champion, 1979).

103. See, in this connection, the important study by Bernard Capelle, 'les oraisons de la messe du saint sacrament', in *Travaux Liturgiques* (Louvain: Abbaye du Mont César, 1967), pp. 242–251.

104. Eucharistic Prayer IV. See the criticque of this by Aidan Kavanagh, a Roman Catholic, in *Worship* 43 (1969) p. 9: 'One who has some acquaintance with the medieval and reformation history of eucharistic controversy will recognize the inadequacy of such a position, and may be forgiven his disappointment that its tendentiousness has got into a Catholic formulary precisely at a time when it could have been diagnosed and avoided most easily.'

105. See Stephen W. Sykes, *The Integrity of Anglicanism* (London: Mowbrays, 1978) pp. 45ff.

106. Christopher Cocksworth, 'Eucharistic Theology', in Stevenson, Spinks (eds), *The Identity of Anglican Worship*, pp 56ff. (whole essay, pp. 49–68).

107. See *Covenant of Grace Renewed* pp. 173ff. See also, in general, Stevenson, *Eucharist and Offering*, esp. pp. 218ff.

108. Henry Chadwick, 'Ministry and Tradition', in *Tradition and Exploration* (Norwich: Canterbury Press, 1994) p. 14.

109. Traherne, *Centuries of Meditations* p. 64 (Century I.85).

Index